HOW TO DRIVE
YOUR WOMAN WILD
IN BED

Also by Graham Masterton

HOW TO DRIVE YOUR MAN WILD IN BED

HOW TO DRIVE YOUR WOMAN WILD IN BED

Graham Masterton

NEXUS

A Nexus Book
Published in 1988
by the Paperback Division of
W. H. Allen & Co. Plc
26 Grand Union Center,
338 Ladbroke Grove, London W10
Reprinted 1988, 1989, 1990

First published by Signet, NAL Penguin Inc, 1987

Printed and bound in Great Britain by
Cox & Wyman Ltd, Reading

ISBN 0 352 32191 1

Published in association with NAL Penguin Inc.

CONTENTS

Introduction

A worried young lady approached me recently and complained that her boyfriend wasn't giving her the sexual satisfaction she felt she deserved. The trouble was, she said, he hadn't been able to locate her G-spot.

I answered her with another question. If her boyfriend hadn't been able to locate her G-spot, why hadn't she simply shown him where it was?

The worried young lady frowned and blushed and then admitted, "Because I don't know where it is, either."

I then realized that ten years after I wrote my first sex guide for men, *How to Be the Perfect Lover*, it was time to take a fresh look at what a man needs to know in order to live up to the ever-increasing expectations that the women in his life have of him. While talking informally to men and women over the past two years about their sexual experiences, I've noticed that most women are now aware that they have an inalienable right to sexual satisfaction. In my opinion that is the single most rewarding result of what we might as well call the Sexual Revolution.

At the same time, however, and as a natural consequence of this newfound awareness, men are finding women more and more difficult to satisfy.

As Dr. Ruth Westheimer recently remarked, "The woman who now feels the right to tell her lover how to stimulate her clitoris just so in order to have an orgasm is not going to give up that right."

And quite right. But this is not the *whole* story. While women may now be insisting that they are entitled to far more pleasure between the sheets, there is not much evidence to suggest that they have acquired an equal amount of skill and knowledge in order to help their lovers to give them that pleasure. (Apart, of course, from knowing what feels good, and having the courage to say "keep on doing it.")

We may have reached the Erotic Eighties, but women still come to me with very basic and fundamental questions about their own anatomy, about menstruation, about vaginal lubrication, about orgasm, and about sexual variations and sexual fantasies. These questions indicate that there may have been a revolution in sexual attitudes, but not in sexual education. I hear the plaintive cry, "I know what *I* want out of sex, but I don't know how to get it together with what *he* wants out of sex."

It seems to me that the sum total of ten years of feminist consciousness raising has been to give women all of the expectations but little of the sexual literacy that should enable them to fulfill those expectations. At the same time, male sex education seems to have accomplished little more than presenting a picture of what women expect from their sex lives that is about as practical as a New York subway map in the middle of Ghana.

The result is that women demand more pleasure without understanding how they're going to achieve it, while men are finding it more and more difficult to deal with their demands.

The anxious appeals that I receive regularly from husbands and lovers would fill Captain Spaulding's cabin-trunk. Although each letter is individual and deals with a different aspect of sex, the basic *cri de coeur* is the same: *How can I satisfy the woman in my life?*

"How can I make absolutely sure that I give my wife a climax every time?" "How do I know if I'm doing oral sex correctly?" "How can I stop myself from climaxing too soon—my wife's beginning to make it clear that she's dissatisfied." "I get the distinct feeling that my girlfriend thinks I'm a dull lover—please help me!"

Now, if most of the wives and girlfriends to whom these appeals refer were as sexually knowledgeable as they ought to be—given what they obviously expect to get out of their sex lives—these anxious husbands and lovers wouldn't be writing to ask for my advice. They wouldn't be anxious at all.

Yet it's not a woman's fault that she hasn't acquired the knowledge and the skill she needs for sexual fulfillment. What is at fault is the contradictory mish-mash of sexual information to which most women are exposed from puberty to menopause. If you were trained to service your car the way women are trained in the subject of sex, you'd probably wind up with the exhaust pipe sticking out of the radiator grille and the steering wheel screwed to the trunk.

Too many women receive only a collection of fragmentary school biology lessons, inaccurate talks from Mom, magazine articles that range from the racy ("How to Make Love to Another Woman's Husband") to the frankly medical ("Pap Smears and You"), as well as a hodgepodge of breakfast-TV discussions by so-called experts who don't know a Bartholin's gland from a sitz bath. It's not surprising that they harbor some pretty extraordinary ideas about sex and what to expect from it. Even educated women discuss contraception and enthusiastically advise couples to use the withdrawal method—pulling the penis out of the vagina on the brink of climax—claiming quite wrongly that there are no spermatozoa in the male pre-ejaculatory fluid.

All of this is not to suggest for one moment that there aren't plenty of women who *are* sexually literate, or that men know any more about sex than women do. I'm not talking sexual discrimination, our sex is cleverer than your sex. Compared with ten years ago, many more women are knowledgeable about their bodies and how to use them, and give as good (and better) than they get. During the course of this book, I'll be talking about what you have to do to satisfy a woman who really knows how to be satisfied, and also about women who are not only sexually well educated but very experienced, and who may actually be frightening for you to take to bed. We can all be frightened.

Most of my recent ground research suggests, however, that the most widespread need is for men to find out how to satisfy their eager and expectant womenfolk *despite* the fact that their eager and expectant womenfolk may not know nearly as much about lovemaking as they should. In other words, what I'm going to be discussing is how you as a man can take control of your sexual relationships so that you not only drive your woman wild in bed, but teach her at the same time how to drive *you* wild in bed.

What we're going to be aiming for is for you to make her feel that you are easily the best lover she's ever had, or is ever likely to have, while you are simultaneously transforming her with your knowledge and skillful technique into the best lover that *you've* ever had.

To that end, I'm going to be talking about what *you* need to know and also what *she* needs to know, and how you can subtly and effectively teach her as you go along. As your sexual relationship develops, she should become better and better not only at giving herself pleasure but at pleasuring you—so believe me, even if you only half succeed, you're in for the sexual time of your life.

There are no sexual politics in the simple fact that physically, psychologically, and for the most part socially, it is the man who holds the joystick in any sexual encounter. As a general rule, he is expected by the woman to control its rhythm and mood, and to possess technical expertise. It is part of what makes a man a man, and an essential ingredient in his attractiveness to women.

For that reason you should never be afraid of

taking control, but at the same time you should know what you're doing when you *do* take control. Somebody once said that making love is about equal in technical difficulty to flying a helicopter—in fact, flying a helicopter is slightly easier because its controls don't suddenly go floppy when you least expect them to.

Men generally have a wider sexual knowledge than women, although both sexes are equally susceptible to sexual myths and misinformation. I can't even count the number of times that I've read in pornographic literature, all the way from the *contes* of the eighteenth century to the ruff stuff of today, that when women climax they ejaculate fluid in quantities that would set the bed floating around the room. Men also have extremely odd notions about contraception and about female anatomy. *Is* an erect nipple a sure sign of sexual arousal? *Does* the clitoris become harder immediately prior to orgasm? Where *is* the clitoris?

To drive your woman wild in bed you need technical information on your sexual organs and how they operate. You also require information on *her* sexual organs and how *they* operate.

You need to know how to stimulate both yourself and her to the best effect. You need to know how to arouse her, how to guide her, how to use sexual variations and erotic fantasies to heighten her excitement.

You have to learn the Ten Greatest Turn-ons and also the Ten Greatest Turn-*offs*. Not only that, you need the ability to get yourself out of trouble if anything goes wrong during your lovemaking—without upsetting your lady. What do you do, for instance, if your erection suddenly dies away, and even humming "The Star-Spangled Banner" won't bring it back? Do you try humming "The Yellow Rose of Texas"? What do you do if you ejaculate far too soon, and she's obviously still hungry for satisfaction? How do you make sure it doesn't happen the next time? What can you do if she never seems to be able to reach a climax?

If you're truly in control of your sexual relationships, you'll be able to handle all of these situations and many other ongoing difficulties without panic (even if you occasionally lack panache). Remember that you have a job not only as a lover but as a teacher, and you can overcome many of your problems by educating the lady in your life. One of the most obvious and enduring myths believed by women is that if a man's erection dies away, he no longer finds his partner sexually attractive. If this happens to you, and you know how to deal with it, you'll not only be doing *her* a favor, you'll be doing *yourself* a favor too.

Because you are a man, because your knowledge and your skill are crucial to the success of your sexual encounters, it is necessary for you to make sure that you clearly know all the fundamental facts about sex, and that you also know as much as any book can ever tell you about the emotional side of sexual relationships.

There is no substitute, of course, for experience, but experience benefits the knowledgeable far more than the not-so-knowledgeable. What is far more important is something that might sound somewhat reactionary, but which ten years of talking to sexually active men and women have shown to be vital in any sexual relationship. That is, one of the keystones in building up a relationship with today's woman is that old-fashioned thing called *respect.*

Groan! they groaned. This guy's talking like my *mother,* or Dr. Ruth at the very least. Women can't have equal pay and equal rights *and* respect too!

Well, it's arguable that women may have forfeited the right to have doors opened for them or to have seats surrendered for them on the crosstown bus (although you will always hear me argue fiercely in support of these old-world courtesies, if only because they are an acknowledgment of women's femininity and men's masculinity and that is what excellent and stimulating sex is all about). What women have *not* forfeited and will *never* forfeit is the right to have their bodies and their feelings treated with appreciation and honor. A man who fails to respect the emotions and the sensibilities of the women he takes into his bed will ultimately never be doing anything more than masturbating inside of somebody else's body.

But don't get upset about it. You deserve just as much honor and respect from her. You're not a sex object any more than she is.

You will achieve a thousand times more satisfaction and will be able to explore a thousand times further and deeper into the realms of sexual pleasure if you always remain sensitive to your woman's responses. The man who learns to understand not only what his woman says but also what the signals her body transmits mean will be the best kind of lover there is.

Read some of the letters I've received, and see

if you can detect what has gone wrong in these sexual relationships:

"I really want my girlfriend to go down on me. I keep trying to put myself in a position in bed where my cock is close to her lips, but she doesn't seem to take the hint. Once I actually took hold of her hair and tried to push her down there, but she got upset and after that I didn't know what else to do."

"One evening I played my wife an S/M video, because I've always had a mild interest in bondage and that kind of stuff. Well, some turn-on, I don't think. We had the biggest row of our whole married lives and our sex relationship has never been the same since. I'm truly miserable, and my wife thinks I'm some sort of pervert."

"My wife has never let me switch on the lights during lovemaking. In ten years I don't think I've seen her completely naked even once, except in the tub. What can I do?"

"One night I got kind of carried away, and tried to penetrate my girlfriend up the backside. That was virtually the end of our relationship. I hurt her quite badly and she said I was brutal and clumsy and an animal. It's not only broken up our relationship, it's also destroyed my confidence in myself as a lover. I'm afraid the same thing is going to happen again. Yet couples *do* make love by the 'back door,' don't they? What did I do wrong?"

The worries are different, but it's basically the same story. None of these complainants have properly understood that sex isn't simply a case of one person wanting to do something to someone else. As sexual partners they have shown no signs of trying to put themselves inside their women's heads, trying to understand what's going on from the other side of the bed. Almost invariably, men who write to tell me that their wives or girlfriends "won't do this" or "refuse to do that" have never acknowledged that their partner may have fears or inhibitions that in most cases could be overcome by nothing more than a little encouragement and understanding.

These men are so hung up on their *own* sexual urges that they become blinded to the way in which their women are responding. And as a consequence of what they believe to be their partner's sexual "frigidity," they become resentful, frustrated, and sometimes so aggrieved that their relationship is permanently damaged or destroyed.

Too many wives and girlfriends are equally guilty of being unresponsive and of failing to appreciate the strength and urgency of their men's desires. Too many women are too cautious to experiment with sex and too ready to wrinkle up their noses or turn their backs or (worst of all) to laugh. But the plain fact of the matter is that *somebody* has to guide the relationship physically and emotionally, and in order to do so you must start by being understanding, patient, and respectful. That will not diminish your virility in the slightest because only through understanding and patience and respect will you rebuild her confidence in you, and reassure her that you are not going to behave in an angry and threatening manner whenever it comes to doing what you want to do at bedtime.

Don't tell me you've never been angry or threatening about sex. Bears don't fornicate in the forest, either.

Women adore creative and varied sex; women are responsive to erotic fantasies, to sexual make-believe, to stimulating games. Women are also strongly responsive to pornography, although generally they tend to prefer mentally involving pornography such as movies and videos and erotic novels to the more voyeuristic pornography of magazine pictures and drawings.

Certainly your woman has rich and varied desires. But it frequently takes time and understanding for her to feel comfortable about acting out those desires for real—even if it's just between you, her, and your Casio alarm clock. All of us have a deeply rooted fear of losing control of ourselves, even with somebody we love, and also of appearing lewd or ridiculous. For your woman to forget her sexual inhibitions and completely let go—well, that takes care, takes knowledge, and most of all takes respect.

This is Prudence, 28, from Boise, Idaho: "I read a book when I was quite young about slave girls in the harem, and I kind of developed a fantasy about being tied to the bed by my wrists and my ankles while a man made love to me. But I went through two long and serious affairs and one three-year marriage and I was always too shy to mention it. My two lovers and my husband were all the same kind of man. . . . They always did what *they* wanted to do, and of course they turned me on most of the time; I'm not saying that they were lousy in bed or anything like that, but I still kept this fantasy tucked inside of my mind and never came out with it because I was always afraid of what they might say . . . how they might react. I guess more than anything I was afraid they were going to think that I was dirty-minded, some kind of nymphomaniac. Or maybe worst of all that I wasn't satisfied with the way they were making love to me. My husband in particular was very sensitive about his performance in bed. If he ever drank too much and couldn't get it up, he used to jump out of bed and smash his fist against the wall. He used to scare the hell out of me sometimes, although he wasn't violent or anything. But you can understand that he wasn't exactly the kind of guy you'd confide your innermost fantasies to.

"Anyway, it was all different when I met Mark. He's a year younger than me, but he's really got his head together. I mean he's very calm, and he takes an interest in me personally, what I think, what I feel. You meet so many men who talk to you only because they know they can't get you into bed in total silence. I mean, they're not interested in you ás an individual at all, only getting their rocks off. But Mark's different, he shows an interest, and I know that he cares. And one evening he started talking about sexual fantasies, and he told me some of his, like making love on a plane or a train or someplace out in the open where anybody could discover what you were doing at any moment. Then he asked me if *I* had any fantasies, and first of all I said no, but he said everybody has fantasies, they're natural, and in the end I told him. He listened, and then he said, 'Would you like to try it?' He didn't make me feel that I *had* to try it; I mean he said that sometimes it's better if fantasies just *stay* fantasies, you don't have any kind of obligation to act them out.

"But he tied my hands and feet to the bed with scarves, and while I was lying there naked he really acted this slave thing out for me, pretending that he was selling me to all these gawking Arabs as a slave, opening my mouth and saying, 'Look at these firm white teeth,' and squeezing my breasts and saying, 'When did you ever see breasts like these?' He wasn't heavy-handed about it, and a lot of the time we laughed, but we laughed together, you know, it wasn't him laughing at me, and as he went on he started to get really passionate. He opened up my vagina with his fingers, and held out his hand as if he were inviting all these Arabs to come take a close look at me, and even though it was playacting, it really started to turn me on. In the end he said, 'Who will have sex with this slave, to show how well she performs? Anybody!' And then he pretended to be some dumb thief who couldn't even speak, and he stripped off his clothes and got on to the bed and made love to me, and there I was tied by my wrists and my ankles and there was nothing I could do to stop him. The strange thing about it was that I didn't have a climax at the time. I think I was too involved in what was going on. But later on, when we made love just normally, without the scarves, I could think about what we'd done and more often than not, that used to bring me to a climax real quick."

Prudence's lover Mark showed that he respected her from the start—which enabled Prudence to confide her fantasy in him without being frightened that he was going to treat her with ridicule or hostility. Not only that, he managed to act out her fantasy for her with just the right amount of humor and passion, but he never lost sight of the fact that, to her, it was personal and private and very important.

The Sexual Revolution may have brought heightened sexual awareness and greater freedom in discussing sexual topics. What it notably *hasn't* done, however, is help men develop a positive attitude toward women that will bring out the sexual best in both of them.

Just as your attitude is vital to success in a sport or career, it is also important for a successful sexual relationship. Your attitude, however, is not something that you're born with. You develop it through what you hear, what you see, what you experience. You listen to the views of people you respect, you listen to the experts, you look at the world around you, and gradually your attitude takes shape.

What kind of attitude do you have toward women today? To your girlfriend, to your wife, to the girls you would like to have as girlfriends? A man arriving unexpectedly into the present day from the year 1957 by courtesy of *Back to the Future*'s De Lorean would be faced with some extraordinary sexual contradictions.

On the one hand, feminists demand that women should be treated with greater deference. On the other hand, any man can go to his local newsstand and buy a magazine for four dollars in which a pretty young college student openly displays the innermost recesses of her vagina.

On the one hand, women are demanding increased legal protection from sexual harassment. On the other hand, they are behaving with a degree of sexual freedom that would have been unthinkable back in the Norman Rockwell days of 1957.

It isn't any wonder that many of the men who write to me these days are confused and unsure of themselves, and especially unsure of how to approach women without appearing either as Wally Wimp or Mark Macho.

"What am I supposed to do? I'm not a very forthcoming person, and I find it difficult to get girls to respond to me. When they do, they seem to think that I push them too fast into getting serious, and then they cool off me. I regularly buy *Playboy* and *Hustler* and I see these naked girls with their come-on looks, and I keep thinking to myself: Why do *I* never meet any of these girls, why do all the girls I meet seem so standoffish?"

The answer to that plea is *attitude*.

First, you have to make sure that you distinguish between the picture in the magazine and the words that are printed along with them, and the real girl.

I worked for years for *Penthouse* magazine, among others, and of course we posed the models as erotically as possible, and of course the text that we ran alongside the pictures was intended to be seductive and arousing. That was why readers bought the magazine . . . to get a good warm uncomplicated sexual feeling.

But however they appeared in the centerfold, those models were *real* women and mostly they modeled for the magazine simply because they wanted the money and because they liked show-

ing themselves off. And the men who scored
with those models were the men who treated
them just the way that you would treat any
other woman, with interest and care and respect.

The Sexual Revolution has brought uninhib-
ited sexual display for those who want to see it,
but commercial sexual display has about as
little to do with real day-to-day sexual relationships as *A Chorus Line* has with getting regular work in the theater. And the fact that we
can all buy magazines and videos showing naked men and women, doesn't mitigate the need
for mutual respect between the sexes. In today's social circumstances, in fact, respect has
become even more important, because freedom
without respect leads to alienation, isolation, and
the widespread failure of personal relationships.

This book is intended as a guide for men who
want to succeed in their sexual relationships
with women; and I mean *succeed*. Not just get
women into bed, not just make love to them,
but form the kind of sexual relationship that
will make your average pole-into-hole sexual experience pale by comparison.

There are chapters on brief encounters, on
one-night stands, on singles bars, on sexual
affairs that blink on and then blink off again.
After all, you don't necessarily want to form a
long-term relationship with every girl you meet,
and every girl you meet doesn't necessarily want
to form a long-term relationship with you.

But the basis of every truly successful sexual
relationship, no matter how fleeting—no matter if it's five minutes in the backseat of a
taxicab—is still the same. It lies in thinking
not what the woman in your life can do for you,

but what you can do for the woman in your life. In sex, more than any other area of human existence, the more you put into it, the more you get out of it. If you contribute skill, you will get skill back. If you show respect, you will get respect in return.

This is Eddie, a 29-year-old athletics instructor from Van Nuys, California, talking about his relationship with a local dance teacher: "I'd known Carol ever since high school. She was always the pretty blond one, you know, the one with the blue eyes and the big bazooms and the waggling walk—the one that every guy in the whole school went through blazing hoops to score with. She went through boyfriends like some people go through popcorn. By the time she left school I guess she didn't have too much of a reputation, not that she'd ever looked at me. I wasn't exactly Arnold Schwarzenegger in those days.

"Anyway, the funny thing was that last year I met her at a sportswear promotion meeting, and since neither of us really knew anybody else there, we got to talking. I never even thought of scoring with her, if scoring is what you call it when you get to 29 years old. But of course I was older, and a whole lot more sure of myself than when I was at school. I just talked to her like an old school friend, and asked her what she'd been doing, and how she was getting along. And do you know something, it turned out that the class sexpot was a very intelligent, very interesting, very withdrawn person, a person with a whole lot of fantastic qualities that you never would have guessed at if you hadn't bothered to get to know her any more deeply than inside of her pants. In fact she was often lonesome, you know, despite the fact that she never wanted for dates.

"The next day I called her up and asked her if she wanted to come down to the gym where I work and try out some of our new equipment— we've put in some Marcy M/1s and quite a lot of other new stuff. She came during her lunch- break, and all we did was work out together. But I'd brought along a basket of whole-meal sandwiches and a cold bottle of white duck and that was what we had for lunch. By then I was beginning to understand what I was doing, you know, what kind of effect I was having on her. She was getting attracted to me because I wasn't pushing her, I wasn't treating her like some kind of a sex object, some kind of inflatable woman. And I sure wasn't treating her like the class whore, either, which is the way that she'd been treated by almost all of the men that she'd met.

"We dated for a week, went to the Getty art gallery, stuff like that, and then I took her up to the park at La Canada for a weekend walk. I guess the atmosphere was just right. I held her hand and then after a while I stopped in the woods and I kissed her. Later on we drove back to my place and we went to bed. Still I didn't push her too hard, that much I'd learned, you know? I kept everything real low-key, real ro- mantic and quiet. I made love to her gentle and slow, tried to take my time, even though her body was something else, I have to tell you, she was so physically beautiful, and it was pretty hard not to get overexcited and kind of juvenile about it—you know wow! what fantastic knockers you've got! that kind of thing. The funny thing about it was that at first it was her who was really uptight, she kept responding like she was acting in a porno movie, you know what I mean, all hip-thrusting and gasping and screaming and all very synthetic. That was what she thought men wanted, and I guess some men do, but it was acting, not making love. Still, I did everything I could to calm her down, relax her, and after a while we began to make love like two parts of the same well-oiled machine.

"I guess we stayed together for six months, on and off. In the end we parted because we parted. But we parted friends, good friends. She used to tell me that she'd never had an orgasm with a man before she met me. Well, I don't know whether I truly believe that or not, I think she was just trying to be complimentary, but I knew what she was trying to say. You can fuck like Tarzan, you can swing off the chandelier, you can get it up nine times a night. But none of that is any kind of substitute for friendship and understanding, and listening to what a girl's got to say."

Eddie used his common sense to build an extremely intense and satisfying relationship with a girl whose provocative looks and promiscuous behavior had led most of her previous lovers to treat her as a sexual stereotype. He took the trouble to look beneath the surface, and he was generously rewarded. One more proof of the point that I have been making: that living in a more sexually demonstrative society doesn't remove the obligation, or indeed the *necessity*, for mutual respect and understanding.

You'll also notice that Eddie made a point of

gently correcting Carol's sexual technique, too. She was bumping and grinding in an effort to meet what she believed to be the sexual expectations of the men she had slept with previously, and up until she went to bed with Eddie, the men she had slept with had either been too selfish or too ignorant to put her right. She had probably been shown a sex video and believed at the time that she was being given a demonstration of the proper way to make love—without having it pointed out to her that the fornication you see in sex videos is deliberately exaggerated for the purpose of turning you on, and that the rest of us (thank God) don't have to adopt all those uncomfortable positions because we don't have to worry about some guy with a JVC video camera getting an unobstructed view of our loins.

Sex is the only human activity that requires a very high degree of physical finesse yet which is almost always performed in private. There is no professional training available, even if you're interested, and there are no sexual Olympics at which tyros can learn from the style and technique of acknowledged experts. Making love to a woman is rather like being handed a jai-alai racket and being pushed out on to the court with an admonition to "get on with it and make it good." That is why there is always a place on the bookshelf of even the most experienced and sophisticated lover for a book like this, which brings together the experiences and the difficulties that many different men have encountered over the years in their sexual relationships, and why you should always be alert to any kind of sexual assistance, whether it's a movie, or a magazine article, or a woman's chance remark. There is no shame in picking up sexual advice from whatever source. You wouldn't be embarrassed if somebody gave you tips about wine, or jogging, or how to carve a roasted ptarmigan. You wouldn't feel that you were somehow lacking if somebody told you a way to correct your swing in golf. So there's absolutely no need to feel that there's anything wrong in looking for guidance in sex.

These days, you're going to need particular help with the newly liberated woman. You know the kind. Those outspoken, independent ladies who know what they want out of their sexual relationships and have both a comprehensive knowledge and a sound appreciation of what first-class lovemaking is all about. One of the major difficulties in sexual relationships with women of this ilk is that in achieving sexual self-realization they have sometimes lost sight of their male partner's needs and occasionally his rights as an individual, too. They have become, in fact, the female equivalent of that macho guy with the gold chains in the chest hair. (Incidentally, chest hair is absolutely okay, provided you don't display it in down-to-the-belly-button shirts, but can we please now dispense with the necklace, guys? I mean, please?) These independent ladies know that they want (and are entitled to) an orgasm. They know that they want (and are entitled to) plenty of exciting stimulation. They know that they want (and are entitled to) satisfying afterplay if their partner reaches his climax before they do. *But . . .* they do tend to have the disconcerting habit of forgetting that a man has his sexual entitlements, too.

How this happens is quite understandable. When a woman first discovers the pleasures that her own body can and should be giving her, she is just as susceptible to the sin of treating a man like a sex object as a man treating *her* like a sex object. Some women blossom beyond this stage of selfishness through warmth, wisdom, and happy experience. Others become even more self-absorbed, and develop what I call the "bodybuilder" attitude toward their sexual relationships, working harder and harder toward sexual perfection but at the same time becoming more and more deeply wrapped up in their own feelings, their own satisfaction, their own sacred orgasm.

Here's Debbie, 24, a music student from Albany, New York, who was inspired to improve her love life after several sessions with a psychiatrist: "I was only 19, and already I'd been through two totally bad relationships. The first time I'd been sleeping with a married man. He went back to his wife after two months, and he left me feeling completely shattered and unattractive as well as sexually guilty. He never was a good lover; all he ever did was climb on top of me and jump up and down and that was it. Then he used to get out of bed straightaway and call his wife, explaining why he was going to be late that night.

"The second affair was a rebound thing. I went out with a young guy who ran a music store about three blocks from where I lived. He was nice but he was kind of weak and watery. Every time we had sex he kept asking if it was good, you know 'how was it for you, darling?' like he was never sure that he was any good at it. I used to get tired of him asking. In the end he made me pregnant. I had an early abortion but after that I had some sessions with this psychiatrist, and I guess I must have told him that I was off sex forever, because he worked very hard to make me understand that I deserved a good sex life, can you believe it? He said there are so many people out there, men and women, who have really dull, flat sex lives, and they tolerate it year after year, without ever knowing what sex is really all about. He gave me about a ton of books to read, books about women's bodies and women's sexuality and what to expect out of sex, and he really turned me around. I learned how to control my sexual feelings through self-pleasuring, you know? And I learned all about orgasms and how to control them. The first time I went to bed with a man after that, it was something else—well, not compared with the sex I'm having these days, it was just a beginning—but it was mind-blowing compared with what I'd been having before. You wouldn't believe it was the same experience.

"I was able to bring myself to a satisfying orgasm practically every time, and the feelings I had were just sensational. These days, I've trained myself to be able to climax whenever I want to, or almost whenever I want to, by using a special combination of mental self-stimulation and vaginal muscle control. That means if my lover starts coming too quickly, I can usually manage to speed up my climax to match the moment when he does it."

Well—I have to admire Debbie's technical progress. But technical progress isn't everything. Making love isn't a branch of engineering. While her psychiatrist may have done wonders for her technique, he obviously hasn't done anything to get down to the heart of her problem, which is her alienation from men. In spite of her newfound sexual expertise, in spite of her considerable ability in timing her orgasms almost to the split second, she is still as far away from a meaningful sexual relationship as she was before. A rewarding sexual relationship stems from mutual involvement, mutual respect, a whole lot of physical and emotional compromise, and reservoirs of understanding.

Do you think that you could straighten Debbie out? If so, how would you go about it? Would you be strict? Or would you be seductive? Would you punish her until she paid attention to what you wanted, too? Would you try to explain that when you go to bed together, there are two of you, and that you have an equal claim to satisfaction? And how would you do that without turning her off or sounding like a preacher?

There are hundreds of thousands of Debbies out there, sexually active but sexually disenchanted. There are thousands of Carols, too, and Susans, and Mary Beths, and Naomis. The daughters of the sexual revolution, every one of them, full of expectations, full of hope, women who have been told that they have sexual rights but who have no clear idea how those rights can be exercised. That, of course, is where you come in. You, *mon ami*, are going to be their knight in shining armor. Or at least their knight in a Giorgio Armani sports coat.

Nota bene, though, that there are going to be

times when you're going to come across women who expect everything, know everything, and insist you to come up to their four-star sexual standard, and by cracky you're going to have to be good to drive *them* wild in bed.

Here's Sharon, 23, from St. Louis: "I guess you could say that I do expect a whole lot of loving out of any man. I'm good-looking, and I know it. I'm 5-6½, red-haired, 36-23-36. I'm fit, my head is on straight, I don't very often drink liquor and I don't take drugs. I work in a real estate office and my job is as good as any man's. I expect a man to be confident, ambitious, athletic, and romantic too. I expect him to be able to take control of me, and I'm not going to kick back and play dead even if I like him. I also expect him to be able to give me experiences in bed that I've never had before."

Gulppp! What do you do to please a girl like that? What experiences are you going to give her in bed that she's never had before? Could you even match up to the experiences that she has had before?

The answer, in a nutshell, is yes. You're a man, and you have all the necessary equipment to delight any woman. You may not invariably succeed, but then the whole business of sexual relationships has a considerable element of chance, on meeting the right girl at the right time, on mood, on circumstance, on the throw of the emotional dice. However, as long as you have the knowledge, the technique, and the right mental attitude—as long as you can control all those parts of a sexual relationship that *can* be controlled—your chances of satisfying the woman in your life will be increased to the nth power.

Make yourself a pledge. Make up your mind that, from today, you're going to be driving the woman in your life wild in bed. Your wife, your girlfriend, whoever turns you on. Do it tonight. Or, if you can't do it tonight, if you're away on a business trip, or if you haven't yet dated that particular girl, make up your mind that you're going to do it as soon as you conceivably can. Because what we're getting into here is real sexual knowledge, real sexual expertise, and real ways to introduce variations and games into your sex life that will take you way beyond the level of what you've grown to expect from sex, and way beyond the level of what the woman in your life has grown to expect from you.

The good part of your sex life starts here. It's yours, reach out and take it.

Graham Masterton
San Diego, 1986

1.
Are You the Best Lover She's Ever Had?

Somebody once said that the sexual act was like going out for a meal . . . it's only as good as the last time you did it.

But there's another side to that opinion, and that is that all meals are different: Some are plain, some are fancy, some are disappointing, some exceed your wildest expectations. The sexual act is like that, too, and just because you had one meal that wasn't quite as good as you'd hoped for, that doesn't necessarily mean that you'll never go into that restaurant again.

You have to understand right from the outset that a good lover isn't a guy who always gets it right. Nobody alive can *always* get it right, and you can forget about those locker-room stories about guys who can get it up nine times a night and whose ejaculations are supposed to be so copious that even the TVA gets jealous.

A good lover is a lover who can make each sexual act special and memorable . . . a lover who can make his woman feel that he cares about her, even if he can't always rise to the occasion. And the best lover is the lover who does this every single time, and never leaves his woman feeling let-down.

Here's Carly, 25, who works for Pacific Bell in Los Angeles: "I was very attracted to Mike the very first time I saw him. I wouldn't say that he's handsome, but he has just the right combination of looks that have always appealed to me. We met at a vegetarian restaurant, of all places, the Natural Fudge Company on Fountain Avenue, that was in '81, I guess. I was there because I'm a vegetarian, and they used to have some pretty good music and comedians there. Mike was there because he'd been dragged along by a girlfriend from work who was trying to wean him off red meat.

"Anyway, we were sitting pretty close to each other, and when his girlfriend went to the bathroom, he leaned over and asked me if I'd mind trading plates. I'd finished eating already, but he hadn't even started. It was vegetable moussaka, something like that, and he said that he just couldn't eat it, but he didn't want to disappoint his friend.

"Well, that's what we did, and we ended up trading telephone numbers, too. He took me out dancing, and out for dinner, but what was so considerate about him was that whenever we went out to eat he always called the restaurant to make sure that they could fix me a nonmeat special. I mean, with every other guy I'd ever been out with, I'd end up with nothing to eat but the vegetables that came with the meat.

"On our third date he took me back to his house in Westwood and we made love. I can't say that he took me to bed, because we didn't get that far. We went straight into the front door, and then he kicked it shut behind him and started unbuttoning my blouse immediately. I said something like, 'Hold up,' but he said, 'You drive me crazy, you're the most arousing woman I ever met.' And he kissed me like Rudolf Valentino, you know, all mad passionate kisses. But then he slowed up a bit, and I can still remember the way he looked at me, and he was smiling but serious. He said, 'It's true, you drive me crazy.'

"He undressed me real slow. I don't think I'd ever been undressed like that before. He ran his fingers down my back, inside my blouse, and that really made me shiver. Then he took off my bra, but he didn't fumble with it—you know, you get some guys who wrestle with bra-catches as if there's a padlock on them. I have quite large breasts, and he showed me that he liked them by fondling them and kissing my nipples, but he didn't forget about my mouth, like most guys used to, as soon as my bra was off. When a guy does that, you feel like he's only taking you out for the size of your breasts, and sometimes you feel that he wouldn't care if you didn't have a head on top of your body at all.

"Mike laid me down on the rug and loosened my belt and took off my jeans. I wasn't wearing any panties underneath but then I never do. It was then that he quickly stripped off his own clothes so that he was naked. He ran his fingers all over my bare body; the first time he did that it was like electricity, and I kind of opened my legs up expecting him to climb onto me right away. But he held me close, and caressed my breasts, and ran his hand through my hair, and kissed my face, and we rolled over and over on the floor just feeling the warmth and the nakedness of each other.

"At last he touched me between the legs, and the way he did it was so gentle, but strong too, as if he wanted me real bad. He let his finger slip up inside me, and his thumb rub slowly round and round on my clitoris, but very lightly, so that I could scarcely feel it to begin with, but then the feeling gradually built up and it was incredible. I grabbed hold of his shoulders, and said, 'I want you,' and he smiled and kissed me, and said, 'I want you, too,' and do you know something? He was driving me crazy. I didn't want him to stop what he was doing, but at the same time I had a very urgent need to have his cock inside of me.

"By the time he took out his finger and was ready to put himself right inside me, I was so wet and excited that I was actually screaming out loud. Then . . . can you guess what happened? He slid his cock inside me, and he climaxed instantly. I let my head go back on the rug, and I thought, 'Oh, no, I can't bear it.' But you know something, he didn't let it upset him. I mean he must have been upset—well, I know that he was. But he said, 'I must have been too excited. It does happen, from time to time.' And do you know what he did then? He started to massage me with his fingers, and then he went down on me and started to lick me out with his tongue. He was brilliant . . . gentle and quick and very, very sexy . . . and after about four or five minutes I reached a climax . . . and he kept his mouth right over my pussy while I climaxed, and made me climax even more because he kept giving me these little flicks with the tip of his tongue.

"By then he'd gotten hard again, and he made love to me properly—well, you know, with his cock actually inside me. And once I'd recovered from that first climax, the second climax building up was even better. We climaxed almost together, and afterwards we lay on the rug and were completely exhausted. But satisfied, yes. And all because he wasn't embarrassed to say that something had gone wrong . . . that he'd climaxed too soon.

"I'll tell you why I stay with Mike, sexually I mean, quite apart from what he's like as a person. He's always considerate, just like he was that first time. If something goes wrong, he doesn't apologize for it, he just accepts it as part of being human. And he always makes sure that *I'm* satisfied, too."

I'm not suggesting that it's easy to be so emotionally confident and as technically sure of yourself when you make love to a woman as Mike was with Carly. Carly herself was quite a special lady, and her willingness to hang in there and give Mike a chance to make erotic amends for his premature ejaculation showed a lack of self-interest that not all women possess. Many women would have said "ho-hum," put their clothes back on, and taken the first bus home.

Also, different women respond in completely different ways. Some women are very reticent in the early part of a sexual relationship about participating in oral sex, or even allowing their lovers to put their fingers up their vagina. Faced with a woman as shy as this, who believes that the only decent way of making love is the "decent way," even the most skillful of men has his work cut out for him.

Okay, I posed the question: *Are you the best lover she's ever had?* Your reply to that question might have been (a) you bet your life I am; or (b) how can I possibly tell and in any case I don't care anyway because she seems to be satisfied for now; or (c) maybe I am, and maybe I'm not. Hands up who answered (d) no, I'm not. There you are, you see, nobody. Nobody will ever admit that the woman in his life might have had a man who was better.

In a way, this is a good thing. Driving your women wild in bed requires all the self-confidence you can muster, and there's no future in undermining that self-confidence by wondering if Marv ever turned her on more than you. Screw Marv. And Dick. And any other lover she might have had.

The way to make sure that you're the best lover she's ever had is by observing the basic rules of good lovership, and then making sure that you add to your observance of those underlying rules your own particular style and talents, all those sexual nuances that make *your* loving different from any other guy's loving. And better.

What basic rules of good lovership? I hear you pretend not to ask. *And what sexual nuances?* I mean, how can I tell for *sure* that I'm the best lover she ever had?

Most of the basic rules of being a good lover are common sense. For instance: Make sure you don't leave her unsatisfied. Keep your fingernails clipped. Don't force her to take part in sexual acts that she obviously dislikes. Shave before you take her to bed, regardless of the way those guys in "Miami Vice" walk around. Never turn over and go to sleep directly after sex; even if your eyes are closing, make sure that you caress her and tell her how good she was.

Some of the rules are slightly more complicated. Should you expect her to swallow your semen after oral sex? How do you approach her if she has her period? How do you handle the tricky question of sexually transmitted diseases, including AIDS, without sounding like Ben Casey or a total wimp? What do you do if she suggests a threesome, and the other member of the threesome turns out be a guy?

We'll be getting into all of these problems during the course of this book. By the time you've finished reading, I hope that you'll feel fully confident that you are an even better lover than you were before, and much better than any of the other guys your lady has ever known.

As far as your own sexual nuances are concerned, these are simply the physical way in which you express your own personal pleasures and fantasies. The little sexual tricks that will always remind her of you. The way you stimulated the outside of her vagina by pressing your testicles against it during sex. The way you drummed her nipples against the roof of your mouth. The way you kissed her, and gently bit her lower lip. The way you opened the lips of her vagina during oral sex, to delay but also to intensify her impending climax.

The nuances depend on what your sexual tastes happen to be. After all, as respectful and as considerate as you ought to be to the women with whom you share your bed, you still have a 50 percent stake in the pleasure of this experience, and if you have a special liking for massaging your penis between her breasts, or thrusting your curled-up tongue into her vagina, then you ought to be able to satisfy that liking. Your pleasure will give *her* pleasure, provided you're reassuring rather than pushy, and provided what you do is done for her stimulation as well. In other words, you don't massage your penis between her breasts, climax all over her chest, and then hand her a box of Kleenex before going to sleep. And if you think I'm kidding, I most surely am not. Plenty of men still behave like that in bed.

This is Mandy, from Kansas City, a 31-year-old divorced schoolteacher. "I was married when I was 21. I wasn't exactly a virgin, but my father and mother had been very strict with me, and I didn't have much in the way of sexual experience. We used to talk about sex at school, what it was like, whether it hurt, which boy we wanted to take our virginity, and of course we used to read Jacqueline Susann novels. I dated three boys before I was married, one of them seriously. We actually had sex two or three times, but I was terrified of getting pregnant. That was the one warning my mother had always drummed into me, don't get pregnant, don't get pregnant. Well, she was right, of course, but the trouble was she didn't tell me anything about birth control.

"I met Bill and married him within the space

of three months. I think I talked myself into marrying him more because my parents liked him than because I did. He was okay, a good clean insurance executive from good clean Kansas City, Missouri. He had short hair and three blue suits and he liked to play golf. He drove a Honda because he said it gave good gas mileage. He was born old, if you ask me. His musical hero was Warren Zevon, would you believe, and he used to drive around singing, 'hiii-yooo, werewolves of London,' you remember that tune?

"He used to squeeze my breasts and put his hand up my skirt, but we didn't make love until the wedding night. When we did, it was all over in about two or three minutes, even before I'd had the chance to get excited. I can remember lying there in that suite at the Holiday Inn, listening to somebody else's television in the room upstairs, while Bill was snoring away and I was thinking to myself, 'Is that it? Is that what married sex is all about?'

"I tried to tease Bill and tempt him. I tried everything. Sexy underwear, all that kind of stuff. It turned him on, but it never changed the way he made love to me. He seemed to think that so long as *he* was satisfied, everything was all right. I began to get very frustrated and depressed, and I started snapping at my friends and students. I guess the simple fact was that Bill wasn't very interested in sex, except as a necessary bodily function.

"About four years after we married I went to an educational convention in Seattle. It was there that I met David. He was a math teacher from Chicago. I found him very relaxed, very good company. He was married, too, but I found out later that he was pretty much on the verge of divorce. He asked me out to dinner and I guess it was almost inevitable that we went to bed together. He took me back to his hotel room, and we ordered up a bottle of champagne on room service. He kissed me, and he undressed me. I'd never been undressed like that before; he slipped me out of my clothes with such style, no struggling with buttons, nothing like that. Then he laid me down on the bed and I was almost desperate for him by then, but he kept on kissing and caressing me until I was *more* than desperate, I was frantic.

"When he made love to me, he was slow and tender and all the time he kept whispering how beautiful I was, how much I excited him. He kept on and on, and I could tell that he was holding himself back so that it would go on longer. In the end, he said, 'Mandy, I have to,' and I reached down and I held him between his legs with my cupped hand so that I could actually feel him coming. I hadn't managed to reach a climax myself—I think I was too excited and too drunk to concentrate, and I do find that I need to concentrate in order to reach a climax. But when David had finished, he didn't take himself out of me and roll over to sleep, the way I expected him to. He kept himself inside me, despite being soft, and he started to massage my clitoris with his fingers.

"I tried to stop him, but he wouldn't stop. It felt too much like masturbating as far as I was concerned, and I'd done too much masturbating in four years of marriage to Bill. But David went on, and in the end I began to feel that a climax was coming and then I didn't care at all.

It was the first climax that I'd ever had with a man. It was the first time that a man had actually taken the trouble to make sure that I had one. I was devastated afterwards. I burst into tears.

"I managed to see David twice more after that, but I guess the distance between us and the pressures of our own personal problems were too much for us. All the same, David opened my eyes to what sex could be like, and last year I found Jimmy, who is tender and kindhearted and a good lover too. As soon as the last bits and pieces of my divorce are tidied up, we're going to move out to California together, Jimmy and I, and make a new life for ourselves. I know how lucky I am to get a second chance. I know how lucky I am to have discovered how good sex can really be."

Part of the failure of Mandy's sex life with Bill was her own fault. She may have tried to tempt him with "sexy underwear, all that kind of stuff," but it is quite apparent that even after four years of marriage she had not made it sufficiently clear to him that she was dissatisfied. This is one of the perennial problems you will encounter when you are trying to judge whether you're the best lover your woman has ever had: She probably won't tell you until it's too late. Most women prefer not to discuss their previous lovers in a comparative sense, if at all. And even when they *do*, you can't be sure that they're telling you the truth, the whole truth, and nothing but the truth. You can never be sure whether her disparaging remarks about the size of Marv's pecker aren't simply intended to put your mind at rest about the size of your own. And if Jeff was really that clumsy in bed, why did she go on dating him?

Because every woman's sexual tastes and appetites are different, there is no 100 percent fail-safe method of working out if you're the best lover she ever had. But after sending out questionnaires asking women between the ages of 18 and 38 what they considered to be the ideal qualities in a superlative lover, I drew up the following twenty questions, which—provided you answer them with complete truthfulness—will give you a fairly accurate picture of how you rate. The questions are not necessarily in order of importance; but it is essential that you answer all of them, and that you are totally honest with yourself.

How Good A Lover Are You?

1. I always try to ensure that my woman is satisfied after sex. YES/NO.
2. I always talk to my woman during the sexual act, complimenting, flattering, and stimulating her. YES/NO.
3. When necessary, I delay my own climax so that she can get closer to hers. YES/NO.
4. I always caress her breasts during lovemaking. YES/NO.
5. I always undress her before we make love. YES/NO.
6. I am always trying to think of new ways of stimulating her. YES/NO.
7. I often arouse her orally (that is, by licking her sexual organs). YES/NO.

8. I always make sure that there is no possibility of my woman becoming pregnant. YES/NO.

9. I know what my woman's most vivid sexual fantasy is. YES/NO.

10. I would do anything in bed that my woman asked me to do. YES/NO.

11. I have told my woman what sexual variations arouse me the most. YES/NO.

12. I caress and stimulate my woman even when I don't feel like sex. YES/NO.

13. I have made love to her in many different locations (out of doors, for instance, or in front of the fire). YES/NO.

14. When my woman does something that really turns me on, I always let her know. YES/NO.

15. During sex, I always make a point of telling my woman how much I love her. YES/NO.

16. I always make sure that I am well groomed before making love to her. YES/NO.

17. I often kiss my woman and openly show her affection. YES/NO.

18. I know how to stimulate my woman in order to bring her quickly to a climax. YES/NO.

19. My woman is one of my best friends. YES/NO.

20. I am happy to let my woman take a dominant sexual role when she feels like it. YES/NO.

This is by no means a comprehensive investigation into all those qualifications that make a man a top-class lover, but it does analyze quite accurately your attitudes and your expertise. Score one point for every honest YES and no points for every honest NO—although if you have more than four honest NO's, give yourself a bonus point just for being honest.

If you scored 18 or more, it is unlikely that the lady in your life has ever had such a considerate and creative lover (although, of course, there is always room for improvement). If you scored between 15 and 18, you are an A-rated lover, but some of your sexual attitudes may be more than a little selfish. Stop worrying so much about your own pleasure—that will come naturally—and start thinking more seriously about hers.

Those of you who scored between 10 and 15 are sympathetic and trying hard, but not remembering often enough that a woman likes a lot of care and attention during the course of a sexual relationship. You are in danger of letting her feel as if you're using her for your own enjoyment and not much else.

Anyone who scored below 10 is in serious danger of losing his lady to somebody more caring. You have allowed yourself to neglect her both emotionally and physically, and it is time for you to do something drastic. For God's sake take her some flowers when you go home tonight, and tell her you love her. Then take her to bed (or wherever turns you on) and show her that you cannot only *say* that you love her, you can prove it, too.

No matter how badly you scored, however, you can and will improve your sexual technique, provided you are willing to learn those basic rules of being a good lover. Provided you're prepared to be responsive and creative in bed, you can develop into an unforgettable sex partner within a matter of weeks.

Every man has the potential to be sexually superb. All you have to do is make up your mind that if you're not quite the best already, then you're darn well going to be. No matter what your age and physique, no matter whether you're outgoing or shy, there are simple, straightforward ways in which you can improve your sex life beyond all recognition.

Incidentally, a fascinating offshoot of the questionnaire asking women what they considered to be the outstanding qualities of a good lover was that I was able to prepare a Top Ten list of those assets women believe to be most important in men. They were:

1. attractive and interested-looking eyes (!)
2. a clean, good-looking appearance (unwashed hair and scuffed shoes were two major no-nos)
3. a warm and affectionate personality
4. tenderness and courtesy
5. (see, we're halfway through the list already and we still haven't reached the anatomical bits!) the ability to be able to kiss excitingly
6. the ability to make arousing foreplay
7. a good-looking rounded backside (!)
8. plenty of sexual stamina
9. good afterplay technique
10. muscles

My questionnaire covered only women between 18 and 38 and for practical purposes a greater

number of them were college students and professional women than in a demographically reg-
ulated survey. All the same, it's interesting to
note that women are more interested in your
eyes than your pectorals, and that affection
scores well above backsides. The general picture my questionnaire presents of women's sexual priorities is reflected in other nationwide
polls, showing that women's sexual needs tend
to be much more emotional and security-oriented
than men's. You will recall the enormous response that Ann Landers received to her question: Would you prefer your husband simply to
hold you in his arms, or to make love to you?
An overwhelming number of women said they
rated the hug well above the hump.

So that's an important point to bear in mind
when you're trying to prove to your woman that
you're the best lover she's ever likely to find.
Technical skill isn't everything, although it
counts for a lot. It's the *warmth* you display
that will win you the day.

Some men to whom I have been talking about
their sexual difficulties have expressed doubts
that they will ever be able to be better lovers.
It's true that if you harbor doubts about your
sexual prowess, it can be doubly difficult to
improve your technique, since so much of being
a good lover depends on confidence. But if you
take the trouble to smarten up, to broaden your
sexual knowledge, and to study those techniques
that can make you a better man in bed, then
you will eventually find that confidence has come
to settle on your shoulder of its own accord.

Here's Walter, a 42-year-old civil engineer from
Akron, Ohio: "I was married once when I was

27, but the marriage lasted only for three years. One of the problems was, I was away from home a great deal on contractual assignments, and one day I came back two or three days earlier than I had expected and found a strange man sleeping next to my wife. Well, there was a hell of a fight about it, as I expect you can imagine, and both my wife and I said some pretty hurtful things to each other. I called her a whore. She called me a lamebrain. But then she said something that really hurt, something that really cut deep. She said that I was a useless lover, always had been, and that I had never given her any pleasure in bed.

"I don't need to tell you that I was very upset. It's one of the worst things that can happen to you, to be told that you're a dud in bed. And of course I believed it. There was the evidence: My wife had taken a lover because I was sexually uninteresting. I felt very depressed about it for a long time. I was impotent for over a year; I couldn't even arouse myself into an erection by masturbating. I used to go to sex movies in the hope that they would stir me up again, but even though I felt lustful, even though I felt the *need* to make love to a woman, I didn't dare to try, in case my wife turned out to be right. If another woman found me no good in bed, that would be proof positive.

"I spent three solitary years staying away from sexual relationships. They were the loneliest years of my life, believe me. I went to prostitutes two or three times, and the second time I managed an erection, and so I began to understand that I wasn't physically impotent, just emotionally impotent. Things were a little better after that, but not much.

"Then I began to notice a girl who ate lunch in the same drugstore where I normally go for my midday meal. Well, I say girl, she was 33 when I first saw her. She was attractive, though, in a completely different way from my wife. She reminded me of that policewoman in 'Cagney and Lacey'—Tyne Daly. And she always ate alone. So one day I clenched my fists and took a deep breath and went over and asked if I could join her.

"She wasn't very communicative at first, but I kept trying. I didn't push her too hard, because she was obviously lonely like me, you know, she'd kind of retreated into a shell, and once you've retreated into a shell, it's not always easy to stick your neck out again. But the second or third time we had lunch together, she began to open up and tell me about herself. She told me she'd been divorced, too, after a short and pretty miserable marriage. She was working for a dance studio. She had a few friends, but they were mostly girlfriends, and she'd been keeping away from serious relationships with men.

"The long and the short of it was that I asked her to go out to dinner with me, and she accepted. I guess you could say that by normal standards our relationship took a long time to develop; but we were both suffering from the once-bitten-twice-shy syndrome. On the fourth date, though, I asked her to come back to my apartment and listen to some music, and she said yes.

"We sat on the couch listening to Beethoven

and Mozart and drinking wine, and then I leaned over and kissed her. She hesitated just once, and then she kissed me back. We kissed and caressed for a long time, and then I unfastened her dress at the back and helped her to take it off. I was turned on but I was nervous; I just can't tell you how nervous I was. But I made myself take my time—take it slow, think about her—so that I didn't disappoint her.

"Underneath the dress she was wearing a white flower-patterned bra. She's very full-breasted, and I can remember thinking how wide her nipples were, you could see the dark pink color of them right through the bra. And she was wearing panty hose but no panties, so that I could see her pubic hair, very black, the same color as the hair on her head.

"She kissed me and unbuttoned my shirt, and then she ran her hands all over my bare chest. I loosened her bra, and her breasts kind of tumbled out—that's the only way I can describe it, they're so full and heavy. I kissed and stroked her nipples, and then started to roll down her panty hose. She stood up to make it easier for me. I rolled her panty hose down to her ankles and she was standing in front of me completely naked. I can remember grasping the cheeks of her bottom in both hands and pressing my face against her stomach, soft perfumed skin, and then kissing her pubic hair.

"She lifted one foot onto the couch, so that her thighs parted, and I reached around and opened the lips of her vagina with my fingers. Her flesh was dark red and already very slippery because she was aroused. I licked her clitoris, and then plunged my tongue right into her vagina. She tasted sweet and hot, and I was so turned on after all that time without a woman that I can hardly describe it to you.

"I kissed her and licked her vagina until my face was smothered with her juices. She held her lips apart herself and slowly pressed her open vagina against my mouth, round and round, and all the time she was panting and gasping and crying out to herself.

"At last I started to flick at her clitoris in earnest, and she had to lie back on the couch then because the feeling was too much for her to be able to bear when she was standing up. It gave me such a sense of excitement and achievement to know that I was turning her on so much. It took her a long time to come to a climax, and when she did, it seemed to me that it was very subdued, but she was satisfied, and I guess that was all that counted. I took off my clothes, and I can't describe to you how it felt, sliding myself right into her hot juicy vagina. I gave our lovemaking my very best attention, making sure that I kissed her and fondled her breasts and built up a rhythm, you know, until we were making love faster and faster and she was clutching hold of me and crying out loud.

"Afterwards, I thought to myself that was the very best time I'd ever had sexually. And do you know why? Because I didn't think about myself. I didn't think about myself at all, I thought about her. I devoted all my energy and all my attention to making her feel good, and forgot about myself. It was then that I was able to face up to the fact that I had been a boring lover with my ex-wife. But the great part about it was that I had been able to change. You can change yourself sexually, you can get better. I guess it just takes the right attitude."

Walter's sexual revelation was an excellent example of the way in which self-help and positive thinking can improve your love life. But take note that you don't necessarily have to change partners in order to create fresh sexual excitement. Serious reconsideration of the way you are making love to your present partner can produce the same satisfying results. In fact, you can often spice things up far more dramatically with a woman you already know intimately than you can with a total stranger, because a woman you already know intimately will not be *expecting* anything new.

Don't think that because your sexual relationship has been going on for years you can now forget your responsibility to be the best lover she's ever had. You owe it to her and to yourself to get the best out of your sex life. After all, as one sage pointed out, we come this way but once. A good lover doesn't allow himself to fall into predictable sexual habits. Exciting sex is about freshness, and surprise. If you constantly think about new ways to please her in bed, she will quickly respond in kind, and the more enthusiastically she responds, the easier you will find it to be that alltime number-one lover.

Let's get down to those basic rules of good lovership we were talking about. And don't think that just because you're sexually experienced you already know everything there is to know. Nobody is born with sexual knowledge. It's like applied mathematics; it has to be acquired. And unless your sexual education lessons at school were *extremely* comprehensive, and unless you've remembered absolutely everything about them, there are naturally and quite forgivably going to be gaps in what you know about the subject.

For instance, do you know how much semen you should expect to ejaculate after two days without sex? Do you know whether the size of your penis when soft has any relation to its size when hard? Do you know how to prevent yourself from reaching a climax during intercourse with almost 100 percent efficiency?

If you don't, then read on. If you do, then read on anyway, because you're going to find out plenty more.

2.
Your Most Precious Possession and How It Works

There are dozens of names for it, from dong to prong to rocket to plonker. A man's penis is his best friend and his most precious possession. The recent success of the comic books in which a man's penis actually talks back to its owner aptly sums up the psychological relationship most men have with their sexual organs.

But best friends can be taken for granted. And sometimes best friends can turn out to be worst enemies. That is why it is vital for you to know all about your sexual organs, how they work, and what they can and can't be expected to do.

The lover who is not only well equipped but knowledgeable about his equipment is the kind of lover who will always succeed in driving his woman wild in bed.

First of all, you have to have confidence in your sexual organs. I have a whole file of letters in which men have written to me saying, "I can only manage two erections per night. Is there something wrong?" or, "My actual penis is only six inches long when erect. Is this sufficient to satisfy a woman?" or "When I ejaculate, I only ejaculate a very small amount, about a teaspoonful. Is there some way in which I can increase this amount to normal?"

Let's take the last question first. I asked you at the end of the previous chapter how much semen you should expect to ejaculate after two days' sexual abstinence. The answer to that is two milliliters, possibly a little more, which is slightly *less* than a teaspoonful. You're just going to have to forget all those wild claims of "spouting semen" made in pornographic stories and treat them with the ridicule they deserve.

A classic example, from the sex magazine *Playbirds Continental*; "She sucked harder and harder, and then my cock started to jerk, and then I came. The spunk spurted, the spunk flew, the spunk cascaded from my cock and showered in thick hot floods into her mouth. Her eyes went wide, and her cheeks bulged as the spunk built up inside her mouth, and even I was amazed at the huge amount of sperm I was giving her."

As well he might have been. She must have had a mouth tiny enough to merit an entry in the *Guinness Book of Records* for it to "bulge" with two milliliters of fluid.

Then let's take the question of size. It's true that a few men do have very large penises and it is also true that a few men do have very small penises. But the differences that are apparent when these assorted penises are soft become noticeably less marked when they are erect. In other words, smaller penises tend to grow proportionately larger during the process of erection than bigger ones. The average length of the male penis is 6.375 inches, the average girth is 4.12 inches, but these days many sex studies measure the size of the penis by its filling capacity, its volume, which averages 17.25 cubic inches. The best test is whether it satisfies your woman or not, and since most women of sexually active age have vaginas that are elastic enough to accommodate and enjoy penises of wildly varying sizes, the chances are that your penis is more than adequate to drive her wild in bed.

Then, of course, we have the question of how many times a night your penis should successfully rise. Some men can manage it only once. Most can manage it twice, given a respectable interval in between the first act of love and the second. In fact, most could manage it three times if they happened to be awake. But there is no hard-and-fast rule. You can either manage it or you can't. The key point to remember is that most of the erotic stories you read and most of the sexy videos you watch are exaggerated. A writer can boast of as many erections as he likes in a story without even stirring from his chair, and a video camera can always be switched off while our heroic member takes a couple of hours to recover his strength. When *you're* making love, you can't rely on flashbacks and fast-forwards and instant replays. You have to do it live. But as long as you give every act of love the best you've got, you shouldn't be disappointed if you can only manage it once. It's the quality that counts, not the frequency.

Because your sexual organs are so externally obvious, it's easy to forget how complex they are inside, and what extraordinary physical and chemical activity is taking place inside your body every time you make love. That most precious possession, however, is a great deal more than a flagstaff that occasionally goes up and down, and your testicles are a great deal more than a Willie Wonka–style sperm factory.

Let's look at what happens inside your body when you reach a sexual climax, and then we'll be able to follow both the physical and the psychological reactions from the moment that your erection first stirs to the moment when you ejaculate.

Your penis is designed for two purposes: for the passage of urine and for sexual intercourse. In its normal state it is floppy or flaccid and hangs down, but obviously a flaccid down-hanging penis is not suitable for inserting sperm deep inside a woman's body, and so when you are sexually excited your penis grows larger and stiffer and points upward.

It is capable of doing this because it is cunningly constructed of three columns of spongy tissue. On the top and on the sides are two columns called the *corpora cavernosa* (or cavernous bodies) and these are attached at their base to your pelvic bones. Underneath is the smaller column called the *corpus spongiosum* (or porous body), which also forms the helmet-shaped *glans* or head of your penis.

When you start to become sexually excited, the blood vessels leading into all three columns of spongy tissue open up while the blood vessels leading *out* of them are almost completely shut off. The result is that the tissues become greatly swollen, and you have what is referred to in less polite circles as a hard-on.

The reason you have an erection is because your penis has received nervous messages from your spinal cord telling it to hoist the mainsail. But these messages can be set off by all kinds of different stimuli, such as a direct touch on the penis itself, or a touch on any other part of the body, a sight, a smell, a conscious thought. Thoughts alone can produce an erection without any touching whatever; and in the same way thoughts can also inhibit an erection, making it die away.

I will be discussing the full effects of conscious thought on your erections in a later chapter, and introducing a new program of self-training that I believe is capable of improving your sexual self-control to an enormous degree.

When your penis stiffens, its foreskin automatically peels back, baring the head or glans. (That's if you *have* a foreskin, of course; you may have been circumcised.) The glans has a wealth of nerve receptors, especially where it joins the main shaft of your penis, and it is the friction of your woman's vagina, hand, mouth, etc., on these nerve receptors that will eventually bring you to climax.

A brief word in passing about the pros and cons of circumcision. There are cases where it is medically necessary, and of course there are millions more cases where it is practiced for religious reasons, or simply as a social habit. Some men claim that having a circumcised glans improves their sexual sensitivity; others say that it deadens it. As far as it is possible to judge, however, there is no difference between the pleasure that circumcised and uncircumcised men derive from sex, or the time that it takes them to reach a climax. Men who are not circumcised should always make sure that their penises are scrupulously clean underneath their foreskins, but then, 100 percent hygiene is essential for all good lovers all the time.

As you become aroused, you produce a very small quantity of fluid from a little peanut-sized gland way down deep by your pubic bone, Cowper's gland. This fluid lubricates the glans and enhances the sensations you are receiving from it; it also has the effect of neutralizing as it flows through your urethra any chemicals that may be potentially harmful to sperm. There is medical argument about what this fluid actually does, but it has been noticed that it is more likely to be secreted and in greater quantity when you deliberately hold back your urge to have a climax. When you masturbate or when you are being brought to a climax orally, the pre-ejaculatory emission is less likely to appear.

Be warned, though, even the tiniest smidgen of pre-ejaculatory fluid can contain sperms, and it takes only one sperm to make a woman pregnant. At the risk of sounding like the good Dr. Ruth, *always* use a contraceptive unless you are certain that you and your woman would both be happy to be parents.

At last, the friction of your glans against the warm ribbed walls of her vagina is bringing you toward a climax. You start hyperventilating— that is, panting—at a rate of anything up to fifty breaths a minute, compared with your regular fifteen. Your heart starts pumping blood faster and faster through your body, up to a pulse rate of 170, compared with the usual 72. Involuntarily you start thrusting harder and deeper into your woman's vagina, and holding her tighter.

Then you cross the threshold called *ejaculatory inevitability*. That is the moment when you can no longer control your climax. You're going to come, monsieur, whether you want to or not.

Ejaculatory inevitability is reached three or four seconds before your actual ejaculate, and during these three or four seconds your internal sexual organs have to hustle like crazy to produce the finished ejaculate, rather like an oddball collection of short-order cooks trying to put together the perfect pizza at a moment's notice.

Your actual sperms were created in your *testes*, more colloquially known as your balls. Sperm production is a steady, continuous process; immature sperms are created within the tiny tubules with which your testes are packed and then moved as they mature into twenty feet of coiled and countercoiled tubing called the *epididymis*. Here they await the summons.

It takes forty-five days for a sperm to mature, but even when it's grown up it isn't exactly enormous. Its head is a flattish oval measuring four thousandths of a millimeter by two thousandths of a millimeter, and its tail is rarely longer than forty thousandths of a millimeter. In each ejaculation you shoot out anything between 200 and 400 million sperms, but if you ejaculate a second time the same evening, your sperm count will drop dramatically, because your body will be unable to keep up with your demands. That is why couples who are trying for a baby can sometimes accurately be said to be trying too hard. They make love so frequently in their efforts to get pregnant that the husband's sperm count is always well below par.

Common with every other mammal on God's earth that sports balls, your left testis is marginally larger than your right, and may hang lower; but each testis functions equally well, and each testis is capable of producing sufficient sperm on its own, even if you should ever be, uh, *unfortunate* enough to lose one.

As your climax approaches, the sperms hurry from your epididymis along a tube called the *vas deferens* until they reach a wider storage area called the *ampulla.* Simultaneously the prostate gland has been contracting rhythmically and squeezing out seminal fluid. Another secondary sex organ the *seminal vesicle* has also been adding its own fluid to the brew.

Once the component parts of semen are mingled together, it is propelled to the urethral bulb at the root of your penis. This muscular cavity has increased in volume in order to accommodate the semen, and also to be able to force it outward and upward as effectively and as powerfully as possible.

A millisecond before you actually ejaculate, the muscle that controls the flow of urine from your bladder involuntarily squinches itself tight so that no semen will be forced into the bladder and no urine will be ejaculated into your woman. The muscles of the urethral bulb then contract violently, with the effect of a giant eye-dropper, forcing the semen at speeds of more than twenty-eight miles per hour out of your urethra and into your woman's vagina. If she didn't happen to be standing or lying in the way, and you had the wind on your side, it's conceivable that your semen could travel as far as three or four feet.

Once you have ejaculated one load of semen, your penis will usually drain of blood and become flaccid again, although there may be times when you are sufficiently aroused to experience a renewed erection almost immediately. Usually, however, it will take you about ten to fifteen minutes at the least before you are capable of making love a second time, and your woman will probably have even longer to wait for you to perform a third time. In common with all other men, your penis will be unpleasantly sensitive to touch immediately after ejaculation, and you may find it positively irritating if your woman tries rubbing it too hard in order to induce another hard-on.

It is important for you to be able to move smoothly and comparatively quickly into afterplay once you have climaxed, even though you physically won't feel like it and even though you mentally may not feel like it, either. Overcoming what I call Post-Ejaculatory Disinterest is, to me, one of the hallmarks of a caring and skillful lover. I will be explaining in a later chapter what you can do to make the moment *after* you climax even more exciting for the woman in your life than the moment before.

Now, it is crucial for you to understand what happens inside your body during sex because it is difficult to control any mechanism if you don't know how it functions. And by the time you finish this book, you should be able to control your ejaculatory process as finely as you can control your car.

It's time now for some self-examination, along with some self-stimulation. This is slightly less important for men than it is for women, since most men have a pretty good idea of what their sex organs look like, at least by the time they're old enough to read a book like this, whereas many woman are still unfamiliar with the insides of their genitals even after they've become mistresses, wives, and mothers. But it's still surprising what men don't know about their own bodies.

Choose a time for self-examination when you can be alone and undisturbed and also relaxed. Take a warm shower, then settle yourself comfortably in a large armchair or on your bed, naked, and position a lamp somewhere close so that you see your sexual organs clearly. If there is a wall mirror or closet-door mirror available, that's ideal. If not, use the largest hand or shaving mirror you can find. You don't need a magnifying mirror unless you have a serious complex about the size of your penis.

I mentioned earlier, incidentally, that penis size is inconsequential when it comes to judging a man's ability to satisfy women. There is no known correlation between penis size and sex drive. In fact, I have found on several occasions that men who were very generously endowed (and were overweeningly proud of their large penises) were by no means the tremendous lovers they thought themselves to be. Their sexual technique tended to be violent and crude, and they believed (quite erroneously) that their organs were revered by every woman they took to bed. They failed to understand that just because the source of their sexual arousal and satisfaction was centered on their penis, the same was not automatically true for their bed partners.

Good lovership, not size, drives women wild in bed. During the excitement phase of intercourse, when you have been thrusting yourself into your woman for some time, the upper two-thirds of the vagina expands, and so there is far less friction between the penis and the vagina in the area where men with extra-large penises believe they have the edge. The area that really counts is the lower two-thirds of the vagina—which doctors call the *orgasmic platform*. It is here that your woman's most sensitive erotic nerve receptors are located, and as long as your penis actually reaches your body, it's plenty long enough to stir her up a storm. Later we'll see exactly how.

Penis size is not related to your overall physical size, either. Some short men have hefty peckers, some big men have small ones. There are no other telltale clues to the size of a man's penis, either. Penis size is not related to the grandeur of your nose, or your big toe, or any other part of your body.

Absolute proof: If penis size were related to nose size, Barry Manilow would never be able to wear those pants.

Similarly, there is absolutely no correlation between the size of your balls and your sex drive, or your ability to father children. There are some cases in which testes do not descend into the scrotal sac at the onset of puberty, and there are some medical conditions that may affect the size of the testicles. Napoleon, for instance, suffered from crypto-orchism, or atrophied testicles. But undescended testicles can be simply treated by a hormone injection from your doctor, and Napoleon's problem was about as rare as you can get. So even if you imagine that your balls are smaller than they ought to be, it isn't time to thrust your hand into your coat and start retreating from Moscow.

Once you have relaxed in front of your chosen mirror (how about a little mood music, and maybe a drink?) you can start to examine your sexual organs in detail.

Cup your scrotum in one hand (this is the wrinkled bag of soft skin that contains your balls). The skin is darker than your regular skin color, and covered with small bumpy hair follicles. These follicles contain a certain amount of sebum, which is the pale oily substance you will find in the follicles of every hair on your body . . . except that the thinness of the skin on your scrotum makes them visible.

Gently take hold of your testes and feel them. They are about an inch wide and two inches long in the average adult male. Each of them is contained inside a separate compartment, and so there is no possibility of one of them moving across to the other side. Inside the skin of the scrotum the testes are protected by a tough double covering of tissue called the *tunica vaginalis*, and underneath this is a layer of dense fibrous tissue called the *tunica albiginea*.

If you fondle your testes carefully, you should be able to feel the coiled-up epididymis to the rear of each of them. This, you recall, is where newly matured sperms wait for the call of sexual arousal.

Your testes make up only one-thousandth part of your body weight, and yet because of the sex hormones they produce, they confer on your body and your personality everything that makes you a man. That is why you should treat them with such respect. In ancient Rome, such store was placed on manliness that only those with testes could appear before a court of law to give evidence. Hence the word "testimony"—and hence, I guess, the expression "he doesn't have the balls to do it."

Both testes are raised and lowered by a natty little system of muscles. The *dartos muscles* are attached to the inside of your scrotum, and cause the sac itself to shrink or expand. The *cremaster muscles* are attached to the testes themselves, and hike them up out of harm's way in the event of impending damage or of their careless owner turning the shower on to Freeze-Your-Butt-Off when he meant to turn it on to Warm.

The reason you have this extraordinary raising-and-lowering system is because your testes can only produce sperm with maximum efficiency at a temperature of 35°C., or about 95°F. If the internal temperature inside your scrotum rises too high, sperm production slackens. This is why men who are anxious to become fathers are seriously advised to avoid restrictive jockey shorts and pants, and occasionally to sit in a tub of cool water for an hour or two. It will be interesting to see if today's fashion for boxer shorts results in a noticeable population upsurge.

You will already know from experience how sensitive your testes are. Any undue pressure on them causes pain; and men have been known to die from shock after a severe blow to the genitals. If you do happen to suffer a blow to the testes, it is always worth checking with your doctor afterward. Bruised tissues in the testes can bleed into adjacent tissues, which will result in severe swelling of the scrotum, and if left untreated, infertility can result.

Very rarely men suffer from torsion of the testis. That is, one of their balls twists itself around spontaneously, without any obvious cause. The spermatic cord is strangulated, and the experience is usually accompanied by severe pain and even vomiting. More often than not, it rights itself, but occasionally a minor operation is necessary to make sure that it never happens again.

While we're on the subject of ghastly things that can happen to you and your balls, I might mention the word that sends a shiver down the spines of all those men who have young friends or relatives who are prone to school-age sicknesses. That word is "mumps." While it is true that a dose of mumps in an adult male can have the unpleasant side effect of making his testicles inflamed, the chances of your becoming sterile through mumps are about as high as becoming sterile from having your testicles accidentally slammed in a car door. So, no unnecessary panic is called for unless you make a regular habit of slamming your testicles in car doors.

While you are feeling your testes, grope around gently and see if you can locate the spermatic cords that carry the sperms from the epididymis to be mixed with seminal fluid. These are the *vas deferens*, which are surgically cut through and tied when a man has a vasectomy. There is one on each side, below the lower shaft of the penis, and they are about the thickness and consistency of slightly more-than-*al-dente* spaghetti.

You can leave your balls alone for a moment, because we ought now to look directly below your scrotal sac at that slightly humped slightly less hairy area known to medical science as the *perineum*. This area is richly endowed with nerves, and is as erotically sensitive to you as it is to your woman. The interesting thing to know about it is how you can apply stimulation to both sides of it. For this you may need a little petroleum jelly or cream. Simply slide your index finger into your anus (I'm not asking you to do anything that you wouldn't want your woman to do to you) and locate the back of the perineal area through the walls of the rectum. If you tug very gently at the perineum in a regular and insistent rhythm, rotating the ball of your thumb over the nerve endings on the outside surface, you should be rewarded with a few moments of interesting sensations.

You can pause now, go wash your hands, and take a drink. I want to say right away that the anus and anal area play a very significant role in sex. Usually—unless you're just about to visit the bathroom and have what that bawdy French writer Jean Genet described as "a cigar at the tip of my lips"—there is no fecal matter inside the lower part of your rectum. This does not mean, however, that it isn't a happy hunting ground for a whole collection of virulent bacteria and that you shouldn't always observe strict hygiene when playing in the backyard.

Ten years ago, when I wrote *How to Be the Perfect Lover*, AIDS was not a major sexual issue. You could give readers advice on fundamental sexual hygiene without concerning yourself about the possible risk that if they weren't quite as fastidious as they ought to be, if they didn't take all the precautions they might have done, they could conceivably become ex-readers.

But the specter has to be faced, even in a book on erotic pleasure and wildness, because the fear of contracting AIDS from an unfamiliar sex partner is severely inhibiting the nation's free-and-easy sex life, and is giving ammunition aplenty to the likes of Jerry Falwell and the Federation for Decency and all those members of the Moral Majority who are crusading for a return to full-length nightdresses and wholesale censorship of books and magazines and a nationwide life-style that resembles "I Married Joan" not only with the lights on but with the lights off, too.

I shall be discussing AIDS a little later, but remember that it is a blood disease, not a venereal disease, and that while there is still a great deal that researchers have to find out about it, you can take certain straightforward precautions that will protect you from contracting it. Precautions, it's worth adding, that you probably take already.

Now that you're back from the bathroom, your drink freshened up, you can relax on your chair or bed again and examine your penis. It will help you to examine it more easily if it is erect, so stroke it a little in the way that arouses you best. You will clearly see now the urethral opening at the tip of your penis. In women, of course, there are separate openings for the urethra and for the vagina, but we have already discussed how your bladder muscle closes when you are sexually aroused. Try urinating with a full erection and see what happens. Just don't try it in the stall next to me, that's all.

The head of your penis, your glans, is a pale reddish-purplish color. During sexual stimulation it will take on a darker, fiercer red from the effects of the blood that is being pumped into your corpus spongiosum, and from friction with your woman's vagina. There is a thin line of skin just below the urethral opening called the *frenum*, and this is one of the most sensitive spots on the head of your penis. The groove that runs around your penis below the head is called the *coronary sulcus.* Sulcus is doctor-speak for "groove."

While you are examining your penis in this fashion, give it a few gentle jiggles in order to stir a certain amount of erotic feeling. The reason I'm suggesting this is not to give you a free license to jerk off (although I'm sure you hardly need that). What I want you to do is study the *exact* way your hand is grasping your penis.

This is important because unless you know exactly how you like your penis to be played with, you can't expect the woman in your life to be able to discover it for herself, not as accurately as you can. It's remarkable how different men hold their penises in different ways. Some of them grip the shaft as if they're Casey Jones trying to yank the brake lever on the runaway special; others barely touch the shaft at all, but hold the penis around the sulcus, massaging the frenum with their fingertips. It's good to know these medical terms like sulcus, don't you think? Murmur into your woman's ear one night, "Darling, run your tongue around my sulcus . . ." and who knows, she might be so impressed that she'll do it at once.

Other men hold their penis reversed, with the thumb nearest the base, tugging themselves off with a gesture reminiscent of the "parade-ground smoke," in which an illicit cigarette was concealed in the cupped palm. Are soldiers more likely to masturbate like this than civilians? There's yet another fascinating and unstudied area of sexual research.

You should now masturbate faster, and harder, but take care to notice if you change your hand position at all as the intensity of your sexual arousal increases. A way of holding your penis that was quite comfortable and stimulating at the beginning can occasionally become irritating—either because you are touching the nerve receptors too forcefully, or because you are not touching them forcefully enough. There are few experiences more frustrating than having your woman masturbating you madly, panting and shrieking and throwing herself around, but entirely missing the nerve receptors around the glans that could bring you to a climax. In the middle of all that, how can you possibly clear your throat and say, "Excuse me, my dear, but you're doing that all wrong. Let me show you"?

As you masturbate yourself toward a climax (well, there's no point in stopping now) notice the physical changes that are taking place.

Your breathing becomes faster and shallower. Your heart starts to pound. Your skin becomes flushed, especially your penis and your chest. If you bring yourself almost to the point of ejaculatory inevitability and then calm down and delay it for a while, you will almost certainly notice the appearance of a small quantity of clear glistening pre-ejaculatory fluid out of your urethral opening. It's even possible to ejaculate a drop or two of semen proper before you reach the point where wild horses and the Twentieth Century Limited couldn't hold you back.

Keep watching your hand movements right up to the moment of climax. It's astonishing to me how few men can describe off the top of their heads exactly how they hold their penises during masturbation, even single men who masturbate quite frequently. Make an effort, too, to feel the various internal processes that precede your climax. You should be able to faintly sense the muscular contractions that deliver the semen to the ampulla, and the filling of the bulblike cavity at the base of your urethra. If you can consciously feel these procedures during sexual self-stimulation, you should be well on the way to controlling yourself like a true expert during intercourse.

3.
What Does Your Woman Expect to Get Out of You in Bed?

And the answer isn't just two milliliters of semen, either. However straightforward and candid you consider your relationship with your woman to be, however much of a honey she is, her expectations are (a) strong; (b) varied; and (c) many. Sometimes they're contradictory too, or apparently contradictory. She'll push you away when you make advances, and then complain that you never make love to her enough.

She'll want romance, glamour, humor, stimulation, respect, domination, warmth, meaning, tenderness, brutality, sensible conversation, foreplay, afterplay, fingerplay, toeplay, full powerful intercourse, a multiple orgasm, followed by a chilled glass of Pommery champagne and an immediate repeat performance.

Mind you, she'll never *tell* you any of this. You're supposed to guess. I think one of the most plaintive cries of modern American sex must be, "What do you think I am, a mind reader?"

Thousands of sexual relationships go awry not because of sexual incompatibility, not because of emotional incompatibility, not even because the couple don't happen to like each other very much, but simply because they haven't explained to each other what they expect out of sex. The pattern is wearyingly familiar, and yet it could so easily be avoided if men and women learned to *talk* to each other about sex.

The trouble is, a dissatisfied woman may go on year after year accepting her husband's inadequate lovemaking, never daring to tell him what's wrong, and if she *does* find a man who makes love to her the way she likes, her marriage will have already suffered severe or terminal damage before the husband wakes up to the fact that he hasn't exactly been screwing up a storm all these years. The wife will have found herself a man who makes love to her better, and will be reluctant to let him go—even if her husband gives the Scout salute and promises to caress her nipples more sensually. For his part, the husband will have suffered the not inconsiderable indignity of losing his wife's sexual affections to another guy.

The lack of sexual communication even between warm and affectionate couples who know each other's tastes and feelings extremely well is sometimes staggering. This is Phil, 36, a senior lecturer at UCLA: "I always considered that my marriage to Kate was one of the star marriages of all time, you know? The ideal couple, compatible in every conceivable way. My field is business studies, and she used to work for a while for a brokerage company, and so we could talk for hours about business and investment and the stock market. She was pretty, I loved her, and we had ourselves a handsome spacious house, and all the good friends that anybody could wish for. I always used to think that our sex life was pretty good. I've always been physically fit, I run, I play tennis, I swim every night. The very first time that Kate and I went to bed together we had a hell of a romp. I'll never forget that evening. Her parents had gone away for the weekend, and so she invited me round. She must have been, what, 23 then. A very pretty girl, blond hair, suntanned, quite small, blue eyes, the little Californian dream you could have called her. She cooked me supper, steaks and shrimp, and then we went outside on the porch for a while and drank some Zinfandel, and she played her guitar for me and sang a couple of silly songs. Then I kissed her and we didn't stop kissing until we were leaping into her parents' bed. She wore this blue-and-white checkered shirt, and tight blue jeans—I'll never forget those tight blue jeans, they were really something, you would have thought that she'd painted her bare bottom blue. I peeled her out of the jeans, pulled her out of that blouse, and then I ripped my own clothes off so quick you would have thought I was Clark Kent changing into Superman. I'll never forget it, I mean that. She was lying on her parents' bed with the lamplight shining on her, naked and suntanned all over, tiny breasts with dark suntanned nipples, and just a little bit of blond fuzz over her pussy, and I climbed on that bed and I lifted her up onto my thighs—she was so light I could always pick her right up—and I opened up her pussy with one hand and I rammed my cock up there like it was a Polaris missile. Do you know, she screamed out loud, and she dug her nails in my back, and without being too crude about it I fucked her and fucked her until she didn't know what the hell was happening. Her juice was running over my balls like a river, I swear to God, and when I finally reached the Big Climax I was thrusting her up and down on my cock, right up in the air, then right back down onto it again, and the cum was flying in all directions. Now, that was the way I fucked her that very first time; and that was the way I fucked her every time. She loved it. She screamed out loud every single time. I mean I was an active, aggressive lover. I wasn't one of these wimps who lie back and complain because their partner isn't showing any interest. I *make* interest, I'm creative. I'm fit too. I play tennis hard and I run hard and I fuck hard. I put my heart into it. My father was just the same. I can remember when we lived in Westwood when I was a kid, I could sometimes hear him making love to my mother through the wall, and you could hear the bedsprings going like an Olympic trampoline. Would you like some more wine? Yes, same wine, Zinfandel. Bitter memories, hmm? Well, Kate and I were married; she didn't seem to have any problems with sex when we were married, in fact right after the ceremony we went over to my apartment and fucked while the ink was still wet on the marriage papers. And Kate never once told me she was unhappy, or dissatisfied; in fact I'm still inclined to believe that she wasn't actually sexually dissatisfied. I mean I don't really see how that could have been. Maybe it was just one of those emotional turnarounds that women go through, you know, at certain crucial stages in their lives, like when they have babies and when they reach the menopause. She had plenty of good hard fucking, and you can't tell me that any woman could be dissatisfied with that."

It was fascinating to hear how Phil regarded sex as a purely physical activity like jogging or weight lifting—a physical activity that always had to be performed right to the limit. He was aware that women have "emotional problems," but—like far too many men—he had never recognized that women also have strong emotional *needs*. He had been brought up to believe (because of his father's aggressive method of making love to his mother) that sex was something a man did for his own bodily satisfaction and that women automatically enjoyed being used as an accessory to help him achieve that satisfaction. He had treated his wife like a piece of gymnasium equipment but he still couldn't believe that she had been sexually dissatisfied.

Here's Kate herself, talking about a week later (although she was a great deal more reluctant to discuss her sex life than Phil had been—to her, it had been no source of pride or achievement). "Phil was a good-looking man with a very good brain. He could be funny and charming and extremely persuasive. He was always good company, very gregarious, very outgoing. Just the man to have on your arm at a tennis tournament or a faculty cookout. Very sociable, and very acceptable.

"Yes, I remember the first time we made love

together very well. What did I think about it? I was—what? What's the word for it? I don't know, I think the only word you could use would be 'flabbergasted.' He threw me on the bed as if he were Tarzan, and tugged off all of my clothes, and then he took off his own clothes so fast it was almost like he was trying to beat the world record. He was always so quick about making love. He took hold of me and virtually lifted me right up in the air as if I were a child, and then he pushed himself right up me, with hardly any loveplay or any preliminaries or anything. I guess it wasn't so bad the first time. In fact, it was pretty exciting. It's only when I look back on it now after *years* of having him make love to me the same way every single time that it seems inadequate and offputting.

"He could have been a superb lover. He had the body for it. He was a business graduate, so you would have thought that he had the intelligence for it, too. There was so much about him that made him likable, but in the end I was feeling so frustrated that I couldn't take any more of it. Most times after Phil had made love to me, I was left completely unsatisfied. I hadn't even *started* to get turned on. The first time I made love to another man after years of being married to Phil, I burst into tears. I couldn't believe how beautiful sex could be. I kept thinking about all those wasted years."

The story of Phil and Kate carries many important sexual lessons. One is that you should *never* consider marriage if you have any serious doubts about your sexual compatibility with your partner. Better to talk it out first, and make sure that any problems you have can be successfully overcome. In my experience, and in the experience of most of the celebrated sex therapists, sexual problems are never solved by getting married. In fact, they are almost always made worse. A wedding band should represent your joint commitment to an already happy relationship, and a large part of that happy relationship should be happy sex. The words of the wedding ceremony may be time-honored and inspiring, but they are not a magical incantation. They will have no effect whatever on problems of premature ejaculation, frigidity, impotence, or any other sexual complaint. Nor will they turn a clumsy lover into an expert lover overnight. You have been warned.

A second lesson to be learned is never to suffer sexual dissatisfaction in silence, nor to allow any dissatisfaction that your woman may be exhibiting to go without comment. It is quite extraordinary that a man and a woman can go to bed together naked, make love in dozens of shameless and provocative ways, and then find that they are too embarrassed to say to one another that, "Well, *that* didn't quite work, did it?" There is plenty of room for dignity in sexual relationships, but none at all for pride, because pride invariably stands in the way of good communication.

Sometimes you may long for pleasures and experiences to which you can't even put a name. Other times, it's obvious what you're missing, but not at all easy to explain to your woman that your sex life would be so much more exciting *if only* . . .

"I went through six months of agony," I was told by Derek, 27, of Flint, Michigan. "I couldn't find a way of telling Sara that I wanted her to suck my cock. It seems ridiculous now, but I began to get desperate about it. Every time we went to bed I couldn't think of anything else. But then one evening we went to a going-away party, and I got a little drunk, and when we were in bed, I said to Sarah, 'Do you know there's one thing in all the world I'd love to happen?' And she said, 'What?' And I said, 'For you to suck my cock.' And she wasn't upset or offended or anything. She took hold of my cock and stroked it up and down, and then she said, 'You really want me to do that?' And I said, 'Sure, do it,' and before I knew it she took my cock between her lips and started sucking it and licking it and really working on it. She wasn't very experienced, but then I think that girls have a kind of natural talent for cock sucking if they really feel like doing it. Sara was terrific. She sucked me and rubbed me until I had a climax, and then she massaged my sperm all over her face. What I hadn't realized was that sucking my cock was one of her fantasies too. It just needed a word from me to give her the incentive to do it."

Especially in new sexual relationships, a woman may feel that she needs encouragement to be adventurous, even (dare I say it) *permission*. As I have commented before, women are afraid of making fools of themselves in bed, and won't attempt variations like oral sex, not because they don't *want* to do it, or because they don't have erotic fantasies about it, but simply because they don't think they know how to do it well enough and are frightened of appearing clumsy and ridiculous. Not that I have ever met a man who complains about his woman being clumsy and ridiculous when it comes to oral sex. There are highly advanced techniques of fellatio, of course, and some women are better at it than others, but as Derek pointed out, most women seem to have a natural flair for good oral sex, and most of the time the act itself is arousing and erotic enough to satisfy all but the most jaded of men.

This is the third lesson to be learned from the sad story of Phil and Kate. Phil gave Kate no leeway to express her own desires in bed. He overwhelmed her physically and mentally with the sexual equivalent of a Notre Dame touchdown, every time. Just as you shouldn't allow yourself to become dissatisfied by failing to express your desires to the woman in your life, so you should give her room to tell you what *she* wants. Encourage her to talk about what she likes, to tell you when you do something she *doesn't* like. But make it a running dialogue, not just a once-only confess-all session, because both of you will find that your sexual tastes change during the course of your relationship, and that some acts that seemed alarming or unpleasant when you first tried them suddenly take on an unexpected attraction.

Here's Orelia, 21, from Denver: "I was very sexually inexperienced when I first met Charles. He's nine years older than me, and I always used to think of him as very adult and suave. I met him after a college football game, at a restaurant we always go to. He came across and asked me how I'd liked the game. I said fine. We talked a little while, and then he invited me out for lunch the following day, which was the first time that any man had actually invited me out for lunch, you know, apart from meeting a boy at the commissary on campus. So I said okay, and we met. He took me to this devastating restaurant, we had lobster and champagne, and by the time the meal was over I have to tell you that I was his, not just because of the lobster and the champagne but because he was so interesting and so attractive, and so interested in me, too.

"He took me back to his apartment. He put on some really soft mood music and we danced. Then he led me through to the bedroom, and kissed me, and undressed me. He was very gentle but very decisive. He knew what he wanted, and he took it. We lay on the bed and the sun shone through the blinds. I'll always remember the way his body looked, all striped with sunshine. He kissed me and stroked me and then he laid me back and climbed on top of me and started to make love to me. He was very easy and gentle, and I absolutely basked in it. But then, when we started making love harder, he reached around and opened up the cheeks of my bottom with his hands and started touching my bottom, you know my anus. Well, I recoiled, you know, because nobody had ever touched me there before, not like that.

"He took his fingers away, but later on he brought them back again, just when I was coming close to my climax, and he actually pushed his fingertip right inside me. That put me off completely. I mean I really went off the boil, and I began to feel frustrated and confused and threatened. But he said, 'Didn't anyone ever do that to you before?' and when I said no, he said, 'Okay, we won't do it, but one day, when you're ready, ask me, and we'll do it.'

"And do you know something, about six or seven months later, when we were making love, he started caressing my bottom again, and I knew then that I trusted him to do whatever he wanted to do, and I pushed my bottom against his hand, and he understood that I was saying yes. He wet his finger with all the juices out of my pussy, and then he slipped it right up inside my ass, so that he was stroking his cock right through the skin between my pussy and my ass, and the feeling he gave me was quite fantastic, and this time I didn't recoil or anything. I actually wanted him to do it."

Charles was patient and sensitive, and didn't persist with this particular sexual technique (which, incidentally, is known in the trade as "postilioning") until he felt that Orelia was ready for it. It's a common sexual technique, a simple way of enhancing intercourse, but Charles didn't make Orelia feel guilty or inadequate because she didn't like it. He simply waited until he judged that the moment was right, and tried it again, and what at first had seemed to Orelia to be "kinky" and unpleasant suddenly appeared in a new and exciting light. The reason? She had learned to trust him.

As Orelia said, "I expect a man to take the lead. I expect him to take charge. If he wants to do something in bed, I expect him to try it. If I say no the first time, I expect him to try again. I don't expect a man to give up simply because I'm nervous and inexperienced."

While I was researching this book, I talked to more than five hundred American women of varied ages about what they expected out of their man when they went to bed.

The results of my survey are by no means scientifically conclusive. For that, I would need to interview literally millions of women. But a sample of five hundred outlines general trends, particularly if the women have been selected (as these were) from a wide spectrum of social and cultural backgrounds, from White Anglo-Saxon Protestant wives in stable middle-class communities to teenage Puerto Rican girls in urban ghettos. Their views of love and sex are equally valid, and together they present a fascinating picture of what today's woman wants out of her man in bed.

I've arranged the women's responses in the form of a Top Ten, according to the number of women who chose a particular sexual asset.

The question: *What do you expect out of a man when he takes you to bed?*

1. **Kissing:** kissing more than anything—on the lips, on the hair, on the breasts, on the body, everywhere. So many women complain that their lovers never kiss them. "He treats me like a sex object, a hole that he can use to turn himself on. Sometimes I feel like taking a good book to bed and just letting him get on with it."

2. **Talking:** few women are enamored of the strong silent type, the man who makes love and never says a word. When you're making love, let your partner know how you feel. Be flattering, romantic, arousing, and encouraging. Every woman

likes to be complimented on the way she looks, the way she feels, and on what a good lover she is. It's also complimentary for a woman to know that she's having a stimulating effect on you, so tell her so. Many women find that a little dirty talk is exciting, too, especially when they're nearing their climax, although obscenities should be used with care. There are women who find them distinctly offputting.

3. **Caressing:** and not just caressing those essential organs. Caressing hair, neck, face, shoulders, breasts, back, thighs. Making your woman feel as if she's beautiful all over, which she must be or you wouldn't be taking her to bed. Titillating those nerve endings all over her body. Considering how many men rate a woman's breasts as one of her prime sexual attractions, it's extraordinary how many men don't pay sufficient attention to caressing and stimulating their woman's breasts, which after all are so rich in erotic nerve endings that it is quite possible to bring a woman to a climax by caressing her breasts alone. Any woman who has suckled a baby will tell you that stimulation of the breasts brings a direct response from the muscles of the uterus.

4. **Playing:** and by *playing*, most women mean tender, passionate loveplay, and plenty of it. There is a wide gap between a man's sexual responses and a woman's sexual responses. A woman's arousal

depends far more on her total state of mind and on her complete responsiveness to her partner, and therefore it tends to be slower. A man, on the other hand, can almost immediately be aroused to a very high pitch simply by thinking of making love, or by seeing his woman naked. It is up to the man, therefore, to control his sexual excitement long enough for his woman's state of arousal to equal his. In fact, closing the arousal gap is probably the single most important task that any good lover faces. If more men understood that their women need plenty of slow and exciting foreplay, fewer women would be accused of being frigid, and fewer men would be blamed for the sin of premature ejaculation. As urgent as your sexual feelings are, control them, hold them back, and concentrate on bringing your woman to the same pitch of arousal as you—in fact, higher.

5. **Climax:** Women these days usually expect to reach a climax when a man takes them to bed. With sufficient foreplay, it is quite possible for the two of you to reach a climax simultaneously while making love, although I cannot emphasize strongly enough that however desirable this may be, it is certainly not essential, and most couples lead exciting and satisfying love lives with very few simultaneous climaxes indeed, if any. Fortunately, women are capable of reaching a climax, and then almost immediately reaching a second or a third climax—

unlike men, who enter what is known as a refractory stage after they have ejaculated, and who cannot then respond to sexual stimulation for ten to twenty minutes. Women's multi-orgasmic capability means that you can bring your woman to a climax during loveplay, either with your fingers or with your tongue, and *then* insert your penis into her vagina to bring yourself to a climax, and hopefully her to a second climax. Although you should still try to delay your ejaculation as long as possible in order to give her the maximum penile stimulation you can, you will find that if you do happen to ejaculate more rapidly than you meant to, you will still have satisfied her. The confidence of having made sure that your woman has reached a climax will help you on future occasions to control your ejaculation—since confidence is a large part of control. You will also notice a smile on your woman's face when she wakes up the following morning, and believe me, that can't be bad.

6. **Oral sex:** A very large proportion of the women I talked to expressed an interest in cunnilingus—having their lovers or husbands stimulate their sexual organs with their lips and tongue—but at the same time said that their partners "didn't seem to like the idea," either on the grounds that it wasn't dignified for a man to put his face down between a woman's legs, or because they didn't like the taste of female love juices. Taking

this reluctance up with men, however, I discovered that one of the main reasons why so few of them indulged in cunnilingus was because (like women with fellatio) they weren't sure how to do it properly. Later in this book I have devoted a chapter to cunnilingus, and so you won't be able to complain that you don't know how to do it. As far as dignity is concerned, the only dignity that you need to worry about when you're making love is the dignity of mutually shared delight, and there are few sexual sensations that women find more delightful than being well stimulated by their lover's tongue. As far as the taste is concerned, the flavor of all sexual fluids takes a little getting used to, but if you expect her to swallow your semen, why shouldn't she expect you to drink her vaginal juices?

7. **Good solid f***ing:** Another surprise expectation was straightforward intercourse, good old man-on-top-woman-underneath fucking, starting off slow and then building up to a fast, rhythmic swing. A large proportion of women complained that their lovers kept changing positions, as if they were taking part in a porno video, and that each time they changed position, all the stimulus that had built up during the past few minutes was lost. Some women find they need to concentrate very hard to achieve a climax during intercourse, and that they need a regular unbroken rhythm of

fucking in order for their pleasure to mount and to keep mounting. "The times I've almost been there, teetering right on the brink of an orgasm, and my lover has suddenly taken his cock out and turned me over and started making love to me from a totally different angle. I can't even begin to describe to you how frustrating that is."

8. **Body language:** One way to avoid the frustrations of altered positions is to "read" your woman's body sensitively. Most women complained to a greater or lesser extent that their lovers or husbands were oblivious to the signs they exhibited of approaching orgasm, and did nothing to help them "go over the top." Their men seemed to be so busy conducting themselves athletically and concentrating on their own pleasure that they failed to notice quickened breathing, flushed skin, erect nipples, and even the involuntary tightening of face, hand, and leg muscles during the "plateau phase" that immediately precedes orgasm. Some women said that their lovers didn't even realize that they had climaxed, despite all the spasms and the gasps and the cries of pleasure. Even worse, some men obviously didn't care one way or another. Another complaint about insensitivity to body signals centered on the way in which men failed to realize that their women plainly *didn't* like what they were doing. "One night, when he was giving me head, he bunched

up his whole fist and pushed it right up inside my vagina, and started shoving it in and out. It was very uncomfortable and it hurt. He has hands the size of Rocky IV. I didn't cry out, I didn't want to ruin the moment completely, but I twisted myself away. The trouble was, he didn't understand what I was doing, and he actually came after me, still thrusting his fist right up me. In the end I managed to take hold of his wrist and pull him out of me, but that really put him off, and we finished up a beautiful sexy evening having a terrible argument."

9. **Afterplay:** I received dozens of complaints about what you might call the "turning-over-and-going-straight-to-sleep" syndrome. The fact is, men *do* lose interest in sex the moment they ejaculate. They find stimulation during their refractory period to be irritating or even painful. They can suddenly be overwhelmed by a feeling of satisfied exhaustion (after all, they do have to exert themselves more than women during the act of intercourse). But almost every woman I spoke to complained about the lack of afterplay they were getting from the men with whom they shared their beds. Usually they weren't demanding very much. A cuddle, no more than that, a few affectionate kisses, a gentle stroking of the breasts. Some women expected more. One insisted that her men go down on her after intercourse and lick

her into a last hurrah. "It's extraordinary how quickly this seems to rouse most men back to a second erection," she said. "Then I get a third or even a *fourth* orgasm, all within the space of half an hour." For most women, however, a warm and appreciative embrace and a few words of praise are quite sufficient (because they're so rare). They certainly separate the first-class lover from the Neanderthal humper. Getting your breath back together can be one of the closest moments of sex, the moment when you win over her affections as well as her body, so don't be tempted to leap straight out of bed to make a cup of coffee, and even if you're bursting for a pee, hold it, and make sure she really feels that you not only find her sexually attractive, you *care*.

10. **Morning Glory:** Some people feel more sexually rampant in the evening; others prefer the morning. No definitive nationwide survey shows if women have a preference for early-morning intercourse, but almost all of the women I talked to during my preparation for this book expressed a strong liking for a dawn encore. The two principal reasons seem to be that (a) it's romantic; and (b) it's reassuring. "You've been sleeping together all night, when you wake up beside him there's a wonderful kind of a *shared* feeling, and to make love one more time before you get up to go off to work or wherever you have to go, that's

beautiful." That's Eloise, from Dallas, Pennsylvania. And Noreen, from Niles Center, Illinois, is even franker. "I guess you could say that I have a very romantic, sensual approach to sex. If I spend the night with a guy I really like, I always want to make love just one more time before we have to say good-bye. I like to sit there at work and smell the smell of him on me. Maybe it sounds kind of crude, but I like to go to the powder room ad take down my panties and find that they're all soaked with his come. The feel and the smell of that is very stimulating; and I don't think there's anything shocking in it at all. I want a man to come inside me because I'm fond of him; maybe I love him. There's nothing wrong in appreciating that gift he's given me. Yes, I think it's romantic." As far as *reassurance* is concerned, most women seemed to feel that an act of love first thing in the morning is a little extra proof that what happened last night was not just a flash in the pan, that you weren't blinded by alcohol or unbalanced by lust, that you took her to bed because you *cared*. And there's a lot of truth in what they feel—because first thing in the morning you are no longer lying next to a vamp with carefully brushed hair and immaculate make-up and perfume as sweet as rose bower. You are confronted with a woman who has been strenuously having intercourse for most of the night, and is probably tousled, tired, and looking less than her best. If she still turns you on now, amid the sweaty wrinkled sheets and the abandoned glasses of flat champagne, then she can probably turn you on at *any* time, under any circumstances, and who cares about the immaculate makeup. Just remember, though, before you start feeling pleased and patronizing that you still like her even after her warpaint's smudged—*you* undoubtedly don't look too hot the morning after the night before, with your hair sticking up on one side where you've slept on it, and red-rimmed eyes, and a seven o'clock shadow. So if she does nothing to resist your early advances, *you've* been given some reassurance, too. Here's Alison, a 32-year-old married designer from San Juan Capistrano, California: "Even though we've been married for ten years now, I still occasionally like to wake John up after we've been making love the night before and demand that he make love to me again. The morning is such a warm, private time. Sometimes when he's lying there sleeping, I take hold of his cock and kiss it and put it into my mouth. I like that because he tastes of us, and our lovemaking. I lick him and suck him a little, and usually he starts to stiffen up even before he's properly awake. I make sure that he's really hard, and then I get up and slowly sit on his cock, so that it slides right up me, right to the very end. Then I lean forward and I kiss him to make him open his eyes. Other times, I'll be lying there asleep and I'll suddenly realize that John's licking my pussy, and that's beautiful because I get slowly more and more turned on as I wake up. It's a very gentle feeling, but I also know that I'm going to get made love to for sure."

Your woman may have a different Top Ten of what she expects out of you when you take her to bed. Every woman has her particular sexual tastes and appetites, and her most important preference may be that you switch on the video to watch *Lustful Wenches from Waukegan*, or that you don your galoshes and your maid's uniform. But the Top Ten that I have presented here, in my opinion, is a fairly accurate representation of what most women want. Of course there will always be moments of sheer animal passion, when all that either of you wants is to hurl yourselves straight into the sack and start going at it like a Seal Beach oil pump. But notice how much stress women place on the emotional and the romantic side of their sexual relationships. The need for romance is not a sign of female weakness: it is an essential part of the stimulus women need for fully satisfying sex. And if more men took the trouble to develop and build the emotional side of their sexual relationships, they would discover a far greater intensity of erotic feeling and win a far more exciting response from their partners.

These days (as your typical letter to the "*Playboy* Advisor" tends to show) men are becoming far more alert to their women's all-around expectations. But I have still found a remarkable number of men who may not openly exhibit macho tendencies—they help around the house, sometimes they cook, they treat their women with courtesy and respect—but who sexually still treat their wives or lovers in the old-fashioned way. That is, they have sex with them only when *they* feel like it, with scarcely any foreplay, kissing, talking, or any other display of affection; they climax, they go to sleep, they snore. And in the morning they expect breakfast and even gratitude.

The reason for this disparity in behavior appears to me to be that many men still haven't truly adapted to the Sexual Revolution. They put on a public display of treating their women equally. "Oh, Brad's wonderful, he cooks wonderful Italian food and he sponge-mops the kitchen floor when he's through, and he runs the kids to school every morning." In private, however, and particularly in bed, many of you still behave archaically, treating your ladies as sexual chattels. And the negative side of that— quite apart from the fact that you may not be giving your woman the satisfaction she deserves— is that *you're* not getting the best out of your sex life, either. You have a tigress in your bed, and you're not giving her the chance to show what hot stuff she can be.

You guys come up with a whole barrage of excuses why you're not better lovers. "My partner isn't very responsive." "My partner is usually pretty damn tired after a hard day working/ taking care of the kids/baking cakes." "*I'm* usually pretty damn tired after a hard day working/ drinking that third lunchtime martini/worrying about money." "My partner doesn't like way-out sex." "My partner has never complained so far." "Women don't need sex the way that men do."

I fully understand that some of what I have to say may make you feel a little guilty, and may even make you feel angry with yourself and possibly with your partner too. Traditionally, sex books for men have been full of reassurance and comradely good cheer, all presented in a style that lies halfway between the locker room and the doctor's office—a massage for your sexual ego, along with a few words of common-sense advice about what to do in bed.

But you are a modern man, seeking to have exciting sexual relations with modern women, and the traditional approach is not enough—not to satisfy the women whose expectations we have been discussing in this chapter. From the start I have been talking about a fundamental change in attitude, a respect for the differences in female sexuality, and also a respect for your own sexuality. I have been talking about acquiring an ability not only to give sexual pleasure but to receive it.

This is Tracey, 26, from Darien, Connecticut: "Lew was always a good lover. He was enthusiastic and energetic. He used to give me regular orgasms, and I was always physically satisfied. The trouble was, he never allowed me to be a good lover back. He always had to be in charge. He would never lie back passively and let me make love to him; he always had to be up and at it. I began to feel that I wasn't being permitted to contribute anything to the relationship, and in the end I was convinced that he didn't want me to make love to him. When I told him, he was shocked. He had always been so concerned in making sure that *I* had a good time, that *I* had an orgasm, that he had forgotten about his pleasure, and that pleasing him was a very important part of what pleased me."

In other words, being a good lover doesn't only mean being a good technician. Being a good lover means striking a balance between consideration and selfishness. As I've said before, there are two of you in that sack, and you're half of that two. You're entitled to your share of whatever's going. It's just up to you to make sure that whatever's going is really good.

4.
The Ins and Outs of Your Woman's Body

There are probably more colloquial names for the female sex organs than any other part of the human anatomy. They range from the oddly reverential ("promised land," "heaven's gate") to the quirky ("muff," "poontang") to the downright hostile ("rattlesnake canyon," "snapping turtle"). The most commonly used slang terms are "cunt," "pussy," and "box."

It always interests me to hear what word a man will use to describe a woman's sex organs because his choice of slang will often reveal a great deal about his sexual attitudes. The same is true of women, when talking about their own organs. Few women, however, talk about their vagina with the same kind of affection with which a man talks about his "pecker."

The reason for this, of course, is that women's sexual organs are predominantly *internal* rather than *external*. Men frequently regard a woman's vagina as little more than a "slit" or a "hole," and a very large percentage of women do, too. But this negative view of the vagina is not only physiologically unsound, it makes it much harder for a man (and a woman) to understand what is happening when they make love, and how to improve the style and quality of their sex lives. More than that, it fosters the attitude that during sex the man is doing something positive while the woman is doing nothing but lying back and accepting his prong in her trench, or whatever you want to call it. The antiquity of this sexual attitude is venerable: The very name "vagina" comes from the Roman for "sheath," and far from being a respectable name for a woman's sexual organs, it is in fact bawdy Roman slang on the same level as "crack" and "honeypot."

In the companion book to this one, *More Ways to Drive Your Man Wild in Bed*, I have introduced the idea that a woman should reverse her mental view of her vagina and see it not as a hole but as a positive organ with as much complexity and versatility as the penis. The fact that it is internal is irrelevant. The mouth is internal, and yet we are still able to visualize it as a positive and sensitive part of our bodies.

It is crucial to good sex that you too reverse your idea of the vagina as a slit or a hole and get to know and understand what shape it is, how it is made, what it can do, and how dramatically and positively it functions during sex.

You would be helped considerably if you could persuade the woman in your life to assist you to investigate the complexities of her vagina. If you are careful and tender and treat your investigation as an act of love, you should both enjoy it, as well as learn from it. As I have mentioned, many women have never studied their own sexual organs closely, and harbor as many misconceptions about their own anatomy as men do.

"I was always taught that it was rude and disgusting to look at yourself," said 29-year-old Phyllis, from New York's Greenwich Village. "My mother was very uptight about sex and reproduction, she never discussed it, although just before I went off to college, she gave me a copy of this really ancient book called *What a Young Woman Ought to Know*, which was full of dire warnings about what would happen to you if you masturbated. I was 18, fully grown up, and I didn't have the first idea about my body or how it functioned. It wasn't even as if I was a virgin. I'd actually been to bed two or three times with one of the boys I used to date when I was home, but of course it was dark and I couldn't really see what was going on, and the last thing you're going to do at that age is drag back the sheets and have a good long stare at this boy's thing going in and out, no matter how much you may want to. We'd done human reproduction at school, but that was exactly what it was, reproduction. All sperms and ovaries. Pictures of bodies cut in half so that all you could really see was dissected muscles and spinal columns. Nothing to do with sex, no explanation of how to present yourself sexually to a man.

"It was only when I came back to my room one evening and found my roommate lying naked on her bed with a makeup mirror held between her legs that I actually saw for the first time what a woman's sexual parts must look like to a man. She was trimming her pubic hair so that she could wear her new swimsuit, and she just kept on doing it. She wasn't in the least bit embarrassed, although I can't tell you how much *I* was. In the end, though, she caught me glancing at her, and she said, 'Am I keeping you from your studies?' and I said, 'No, of course not, but—'well, I said something like, 'I never could have done that at home.' I can't remember exactly what. And Donna, that was her name, she was curious at first, and then she was amazed, and in the end she told me to come over, and I sat on the end of the bed while she stretched her legs open and showed me her vagina, quite openly, and she told me so much about myself sexually, even though she wasn't any kind of an expert, she just knew her body, she knew herself as a woman. She made me touch her clitoris so that I could feel it for myself, and then she took my fingers and slipped them inside her so that I could feel everything that she was talking about. There wasn't anything lesbian about it, it was just somebody revealing a physical mystery—and, believe me, after that, my whole attitude to myself and my sexuality was different. My whole attitude to sex was different."

If you don't have your woman immediately to hand in order to help you out, then you can treat this chapter as a dry run. Later, when you're together again, you can run through it for real from memory. It won't matter if you don't want to tell her that you're exploring her body; this particular exploration can double as foreplay, and she should enjoy it just as much as your regular foreplay. If not more so.

When a woman opens her thighs, what you see at first are the external sexual organs, known altogether as the *vulva*. At the top of the vulva is the plump pad of tissue known as the *mons veneris*, or mound of Venus. From each side of this mound, two fleshy folds of skin extend downward to meet again at the perineal area, just in front of the anus. These folds of skin are known as the *labia majora*, or larger lips. At puberty a woman grows hair on the mound of Venus and on the outer surfaces of the labia majora. The inside surfaces are kept moist by sweat glands and sebaceous glands.

Gently part the labia majora with your fingers, and inside you will see the delicate *labia minora*, or small lips, which protect the actual opening of the vagina. Some women have quite small labia minora, others have much more fleshy and pendulous ones. There is no sexual difference between them, although some men have an erotic preference for women with prominent vaginal lips.

Peel apart the labia minora with the tip of your finger and slide it upward until you reach the little pink nib of flesh in the front, over which the two lips join to form a hood of skin. This is the *clitoris*, the most erotically sensitive spot in a woman's body. It is the exact equivalent of the male penis, although of course it is much smaller. In the human embryo, the clitoris and the penis are developed from the same tissues; and like the penis, the clitoris is served by a wealth of blood vessels. Like the penis, it becomes erect during sexual excitement. You should try to stiffen it now (if it isn't already) by carefully manipulating it with your fingertips.

A very soft, insistent "strumming," just above the peak of the clitoris, is usually the most immediately pleasurable.

Below the clitoris (if you can tear yourself away for a moment) you will find the small urethral opening, from which your woman urinates. It is worth mentioning at this point that some women masturbate by inserting objects into their urethras, such as Q-tips greased with petroleum jelly, or even ball-point pens. They are ill advised to do so, because of the risk of tearing the sensitive tissues and also of losing some of the objects inside the bladder. You would be equally ill-advised to attempt to arouse your woman by inserting anything—absolutely anything—into her urethra. The only possible exception is the very tip of your tongue, a sensation some women find uncomfortable but others find "shiveringly pleasurable."

Well, all right, you can caress the clitoris a little longer if you want to. You will have noticed how stiff and aroused it has become, almost like the beak of a small bird. Only your woman can tell you precisely how she enjoys her clitoris being stroked the most, but the structure of it does indicate that a quick, light caressing of the shaft just a smidgen above the tip, coupled with an occasional circle around the tip itself with well-lubricated fingers, is most likely to bring the best results. Some women like to have the whole of the surrounding area caressed as well, giving a more general massage to the vulva, but again this is something you will have to determine from your lady love by trial and, I hope, not too many errors.

Now you can run your finger back down the

parted labia minora to the vaginal opening itself. If you have been caressing successfully,
the vagina should be quite moist by now. In
virgins the opening of the vagina is sometimes
partially closed by a thin membrane called the
hymen, or maidenhead. Although some girls
occasionally have a rather tough hymen, it is
almost always broken during the first act of
intercourse, and only rarely with the pain and
bleeding associated with romantic movies. These
days it is becoming rare to find a girl with an
unbroken hymen, either because it has been
broken by masturbating with phallic objects, or
more commonly because of the insertion of tam-
pons during her period. Strenuous physical exercise like jogging or cycling can also rupture
the hymen.

The vagina itself is a muscular "barrel" about
ten centimeters long, angled upward into the
body at approximately 65 degrees, which cor-
responds closely to the angle at which the erect
male penis stands up. If you open the vaginal
entrance and stretch it apart a little, you will
see that its lining is pink and glistening, and
that it has ribs or folds. These folds (called
rugae) are much more pronounced in young
women; as a woman grows older they gradually
disappear.

Normally the front wall and the back wall of
the vagina rest closely together, but they are
easily parted and stretched during sexual intercourse. Insert two fingers into your woman's
vagina and open them out like a pair of scissors, and you will feel for yourself how elastic
her vagina actually is. A measure of the vagina's versatility is that (apart from stretching

wide enough to give birth) one of the girls I talked to while preparing this book could raise and lower an object as large as a 7-Up bottle and an object as slim as a pencil using her vaginal muscles alone. Quite a rare talent, and not particularly recommended (the best foreign body that a woman can introduce into her vagina is a male penis). But all the same, it is a vivid illustration of the vagina as a positive rather than a negative organ.

Ask your lady to test the muscularity of her vagina by gripping your single finger. With practice, she should be able to hold it quite tightly.

If you probe deeper into the vagina, you will first of all reach a small chamber called the *anterior fornix*. Immediately behind it you will be able to feel the muscular *cervix*, or neck of the womb. The cervix is extremely sensitive, and some women find that the sensation of their partner's penis thrusting against it during intercourse in certain positions is uncomfortable or even painful. Many women, however, derive a great deal of pleasure from the sensation, and more than one woman I interviewed expressed a liking when being masturbated or licked by her lover for having the neck of her womb grasped in his fingers and gently and rhythmically "stirred."

Behind the neck of the womb is another chamber called the *posterior fornix*. During the final stages of intercourse, these chambers expand, so that when you ejaculate they form a "pool" of semen into which the neck of the womb directly dips.

Throughout this intimate investigation of your woman's vagina, I have emphasized the word "gentle" again and again. The vaginal lining is delicate and sensitive, and the sexual respect you show for your woman should include careful physical handling and very well-trimmed fingernails. This is not to say that there aren't moments when a woman doesn't enjoy sex that is a little rougher than usual or having the lips of her vagina stretched open during moments of high sexual excitement. But it does mean that you *never* scratch her, and never actually hurt her. That's one of the unshakable rules of being a good lover. If you want to hurt somebody, go down to the gym and do some sparring.

Some women, either when they're alone or when they're in bed with their lovers, enjoy the use of a vibrator. In case you're one of the three men in the world who has never seen one, a vibrator is a rocket-shaped plastic object that bears an extraordinary dimensional kinship to the male penis. It contains a small battery-operated electrical motor that spins an eccentric weight around and around, setting up a buzzing vibration. Some vibrators come equipped with molded latex sleeves that can be slipped over them to heighten their similarity to the male penis—complete with a knobby end, thick veins down the sides, and (occasionally) a reproduction scrotum.

I recommended the use of a vibrator to a young lady from St. Paul, Minnesota, named Michelle, who wrote that she found it impossible to visualize her vagina as anything but a hole. Her difficulty wasn't helped by her husband, whose lovemaking was perfunctory and who treated her sexual organs (in her words) as "a handy place to get his rocks off, and that's all."

Apart from the sexual satisfaction the vibrator gave her, thus calming her immediate sense of frustration and sexual urgency, it enabled her to explore at her own pace the length and breadth of her vagina, to understand what sensations it was capable of giving her, how long it usually took her to reach a climax, and which sexual positions gave her the most enjoyment. For the first time in her life she was able to achieve a multiple orgasm—that is, a series of three or four orgasms one after the other. At last she came to realize what a strong and versatile organ her vagina was, to visualize it mentally as it went through all the changes of sexual arousal, and to be able to say to her husband "don't do it this way—I prefer it this way" and derive the maximum enjoyment from making love.

The result: Her obvious enjoyment improved her husband's enjoyment, and his lovemaking became almost twice as frequent and "more than a hundred times more exciting."

Here's what Michelle said: "In the afternoon when I know I'm not going to be disturbed I undress and take a shower. Then I go to the bedroom and lie down naked on the bed. I massage myself with a little body cream, arms, legs, and stomach, and then getting around to the breasts, flicking my nipples with my fingertips to start with, then tugging and twisting them. This isn't something that a man could do, because he would hurt me, but I always like to twist my nipples, it makes them very stiff and it gives me a real good glowing sensation in my breasts.

"I leave the vibrator in the bedside drawer right up until the last possible moment. I guess I like the suspense! I massage my stomach and my thighs, and then I start stroking myself between my legs, squeezing my thighs together and diddling my clitoris. At last, when I'm really turned on, I take the vibrator out of the drawer. It's a big one, a ten-inch one. I can't get it all in me but I think the size of it is very exciting and a little bit threatening. It has a pink rubber cover on it just like a man's cock. I think it's called the Stallion or something like that. I bought it mail-order through a sex magazine. I rub it all over with a little KY jelly until it's slippery and shiny, and then I switch it on. I didn't use to like the noise it made at first, but now I've gotten used to it. Sometimes I play music on the stereo to relax me while I'm doing it, that helps.

"I run the head of the vibrator up and down my slit, and then I push it a little deeper so that it's nuzzling right between my lips. I rub it around and around my clitoris until I start to get a particular tingling feeling. It's half exciting and half irritating. When I start to feel like that, I move the vibrator downward and push it in so that its head is only just inside my vagina. I try to resist pushing the whole length of it inside me as long as I can. I usually watch myself in the mirror on the dressing table when I'm doing this. I like to see my vaginal lips wide open, I hold them open with my fingers, and this huge glistening vibrator with its head buried inside me. I think sex is very visual, you should see what's happening as well as feel it, and ever since I started using this vibrator I've gotten to know what I look like, what my sexual parts look like, and how they change when I get excited.

"Anyway, I massage my clitoris with my fingers, and then I slowly slide the vibrator into my vagina, inch by inch, and I grip it with my muscles all the way. I keep my legs wide open, so that I can push it in as deep as possible. I like it when it goes really deep, with only about an inch of it protruding out of my vagina. I squeeze my vaginal muscles just the way you told me so that I can actually feel the shape of my vagina around the vibrator. Then I slowly slide it out again. I can see then just how much sexual juice is flowing out of me. I never used to realize before that a woman's vagina gets so well lubricated during sex. I like to dip my fingertips into my vagina then so that when I fondle my clitoris it will be truly slippery.

"Then I slide the vibrator back in again and change to my favorite position, which is lying with one knee upward and the other knee lying flat against the bed. I reach around behind me and push the vibrator up from the back, because I like my husband to lie behind me when he's making love to me; that means I can rub my own clitoris while he's doing it and make sure that I reach an orgasm.

"If I push the vibrator deep and slow so that most of the pressure is toward the front of my vagina, I get the best feeling. After that I start to push it in and out quicker and quicker, I can't help myself, and I start rubbing my clitoris fantastically fast. But when I feel the first spasms coming, I deliberately slow myself down, and push the vibrator right up me as far as it will go, and rub my clitoris real slow and easy, until I can hardly stand it.

"I do this four, maybe five times, and then I know that I can't hold it back any longer, and I churn that vibrator round and round inside of me, and I have orgasms like no orgasms I ever had before. Then sometimes I can quiet down a little and start all over again. Sometimes when I'm really feeling hot I like to push the vibrator into my ass. I do that real slow and careful but it can go in very deep, and I get a vibrating feeling that goes right up through my womb and my stomach. I do that slower, in a more meditative kind of way. I lie back on the bed with the vibrator up inside my ass maybe eight or nine inches and I slowly run my fingers very lightly around and around my anus which is very stretched and swollen and red because of the vibrator forced into it but incredibly sensitive; you don't have any idea how sensitive it can get, and all the time the vibrator is giving me these deep deep erotic feelings.

"Sometimes I rub my clitoris, sometimes I don't. Sometimes I just lie back and let the feeling build up and up. Sometimes I slip my fingers up inside my vagina while the vibrator is buried in my bottom, and I can feel the vibrator through the thin skin, and I can take hold of it and churn it around so that it vibrates against my womb right through the skin of my ass. I don't do this too often, but when I do it gives me orgasms like some kind of earthquake, I mean orgasms you could measure on the Richter scale. And it's truly helped me to picture in my mind what my vagina is like. I can describe the shape of it, and how it moves. I feel like I've discovered the true picture of my femininity."

I have quoted Michelle's letter almost in full, even though it is so blatantly exhibitionistic. She obviously found it exciting to describe her activities with the vibrator in such graphic detail, and to try to communicate some kind of word picture of what she looked like while she was masturbating. However, the letter contains several important and serious points, and if Michelle can turn herself on to sex to such a high degree simply by exploring the nature of her own body, then I don't think anybody could argue that she is *entitled* to be exhibitionistic about it.

Much is said about the benefits of female masturbation in improving sexual relationships. Dr. Ruth Westheimer suggests that women should light a candle, get into a tub, sip at a glass of wine, and spend a quiet hour or two playing with themselves—"first to teach *herself* how to have an orgasm in order to teach *him*."

But there is so much more to successful sexual intercourse than having orgasms, as your own lady will tell you. While most men feel chronically frustrated if they fail to reach a climax, most women can enjoy several bouts of intercourse without having an orgasm, provided they feel sexually and emotionally fulfilled. This doesn't relieve you of the duty to ensure that your lady has the most satisfying time imaginable, but it does mean that you don't have to concentrate on hurrying toward a climax, willy-nilly. You should concentrate on making love skillfully, with meaning, and with real appreciation of your lady's body and soul. The climax will come when it feels like it, and the more dedication you have put into achieving it, the more time and care and attention, the more devastating it will be.

Women should masturbate in order to explore their own sexual feelings and their own sexual anatomy. But they shouldn't masturbate with nothing in mind but reaching a climax. If they do, they will be missing all the important lessons that self-stimulation can teach them, the lessons that Michelle points out in her letter with remarkable clarity and self-understanding.

First of all, Michelle indulges in quite elaborate foreplay, massaging herself, gently stimulating her breasts and nipples, and gradually working herself up into a physical and mental state where she is prepared for intercourse (or, in this case, the insertion of a vibrator). She deliberately increases the sexual tension by waiting until the last possible moment before she takes the vibrator out of her bedside drawer. Then she prepares it by smearing it with jelly, a process that serves to excite her even more and to increase her anticipation.

What *you* can learn from that is that suspense can almost always heighten sexuality. No matter how wildly rampant you feel, if you can manage to control your (quite understandable) urge to thrust yourself into your woman at the first possible opportunity—if you can hold your natural instincts back long enough to give her long moments of delirious foreplay—you will find that she is far more responsive to you when you eventually slide your erection in. Far readier for you, too, both physically and emotionally, and that much closer to a climax.

There is nothing wrong with a little ritual in lovemaking, either, provided that ritual doesn't become boring and predictable. The application of petroleum jelly is Michelle's ritual; yours could be anything from the way you unbutton her blouse to a special way of kissing her nipples. A gesture that shows her that she attracts you fiercely, and that you intend to make love to her as skillfully and as meaningfully as you can.

You will notice that Michelle keeps the sexual suspense going even when she has prepared her vibrator for action. She titillates her clitoris with it, and slides it up and down her labia majora. Even when she eventually inserts it into her vagina, she doesn't immediately thrust it right up herself; instead, she teases herself by pushing only the head of it in and holding back her natural urge to push the whole length of it as far up as it will go. This is something that you can do with your penis during intercourse, running the head of it up and down her outer lips, and then sliding only the glans into her vagina, resisting any efforts that your woman might make to pull you fully into herself. Resisting your own urges, too.

Michelle makes an interesting point at this stage. She looks at herself closely in her bedroom mirror, enjoying the sight of her vibrator half inserted into her vulva. The sights of sex are an important stimulus, as well as a valuable education. Even today, after the Sexual Revolution, many couples still make love under the sheets, with the lights switched off, when they could and should be reveling in the sight of their own bodies sexually joined together. As a man, you should encourage your woman to watch your penis sliding into her vagina—either by using mirrors, or more simply by kneeling up with your back straight and opening her thighs wide so that she can see more easily. While you're doing this, incidentally, a few murmured words of appreciation and affection wouldn't go amiss—look at your beautiful pussy, look how hard you've made me, that kind of talk.

At last Michelle pushes her vibrator deeply into herself. She squeezes her muscles around it so that she can feel every inch of it, and that feeling is transmitted to her conscious mind as a picture of what her vagina is like: not just a "hole" or a slit, but an active, receptive organ that is sharing the nervous and muscular activity of lovemaking with the male member that has been inserted into it. In this particular case, of course, the male member is artificial, but Michelle has obviously found that her responses to her husband's penis have improved just as much through the same "imaging" of what her vagina is like in her mind.

By using her vibrator regularly, Michelle has even been able to identify the sexual position that arouses her the most. She lies back with one knee flat sideways on the bed, the other knee raised up at 90 degrees, and she prefers to have her vibrator (or her husband's penis) inserted from behind her.

You may remember at the beginning of this book that I was asked by a young woman where her G-spot was. Well, I have always refuted the existence of a "trigger spot" that can infallibly arouse all women. All women like to be stimulated in different ways, just as men do. Some women like to have their clitoris "mashed" quite fiercely, while for others the very lightest of butterfly touches is enough. Some women can reach orgasm simply by squeezing their thighs together; others need half an hour of concentrated clitoral titillation. But if a woman lies like Michelle, and her lover's penis is inserted from behind, the head of his penis as he thrusts into her will rhythmically compress her internal flesh against her pubic bone and transmit internal pressure to the deeply buried erectile tissues of her clitoris. In other sexual positions, there is usually less transmitted pressure, and that is why Michelle happens to prefer this position. It also has the advantage of allowing her (or her husband) to reach down in front and stimulate her clitoris manually. During face-to-face intercourse, there is no direct stimulation of the clitoris, except if you push yourself very deeply into her and grind your pubic bone against hers. It is the way that your penis tugs on her labia minora that stimulates her clitoris. So, if your woman has difficulty reaching orgasms without direct clitoral touching, the advantages of doing it Michelle's way are obvious.

As I have said, though, it is a mistake to regard orgasm as essential. Time and time again, I receive letters from couples who have obviously been working like Soviet road-menders to achieve a climax. My advice to them is always to relax, to enjoy the act of making love without fretting about climaxes all the time. You'd think that some couples honestly don't like to make love, the way they're so concerned about bringing it to a climax. If you take your time and relish every moment, there will be more tension, more erotic excitement, more pleasure, and far more likelihood of *both* of you reaching a climax.

You can help your woman to understand the nature of her vagina by softly encouraging her to imagine what her vagina is doing when your penis slides into it. You don't have to use technical or medical terms; use whatever language turns you on the most. But when you actually *know* what's happening inside her body second by second and can actually feel and identify the various stages of her sexual excitement, you will find that you have far more confidence in your talents as a lover and that you can help her to enjoy her lovemaking more than she ever thought possible.

In the following chapter we'll take a look at what happens when your woman becomes sexually aroused and what you can do to enhance her pleasure.

A brief word, though, about Michelle's occasional use of her vibrator to stimulate herself anally. The anus, like the vagina, is richly supplied with nerves, and inserting any object into it as large as a ten-inch vibrator is bound to affect the muscles and nerves of what is technically called the "orgasmic platform." There is a long sexual and cultural history to stimulation of the anus with artificial members, and provided great care is taken not to insert anything that might cause damage to the delicate tissues of the rectum or anything that might accidentally become lodged up inside the bowel, it can be a highly erotic form of masturbation. Pauline Reage, in *The Story of O*, mentions that "O wore, inserted in her anus and held in place by three little chains attached to a leather belt encircling her haunches, held, that is to say, in such a manner that the play of her internal muscles was unable to dislodge it, an ebonite rod fashioned in the shape of an uprisen male sex."

During loveplay you may sometimes wish to increase your woman's pleasure by inserting one of your fingers into her anus. Notice that Michelle pressed the head of the vibrator up against the neck of her womb through the skin that separates her vagina from her rectum. If you want to stimulate your woman in the same way, you should insert your finger into her anus right up as far as it will go, and then if you gently press upward and forward, you should be able to feel the muscular cervix. A gentle rotating motion of your fingertip around the neck of the womb will stimulate not only her womb, but her vagina, anus, and perineum. As Michelle says, "It gives me orgasms you could measure on the Richter scale." (Remember, though, to keep those fingernails very closely trimmed and not to insert the same finger into your woman's vagina until you have washed it thoroughly. There is rarely any fecal matter in the rectum, but malevolent bacteria abound.)

Let's take an internal look now at what actually happens when you turn your woman on . . . and how you can make sure that she remembers your lovemaking forever.

5.
The Rise and Rise of Your Woman's Excitement

We have Masters and Johnson to thank for much of our understanding of what happens inside a woman's body when she becomes sexually aroused. Although many of their studies have been criticized lately for an alleged lack of scientific control, their insight into the physical changes that take place inside the body was unprecedented, and has contributed enormously to our understanding of how we make love and how we can make love *better*.

When you first excite your woman by kissing her and caressing her, her body undergoes certain physical changes, just as yours does. The most noticeable physical change *you* go through is the erection of your penis. This swelling of the sexual organs with blood is called *vasocongestion*, but it doesn't happen only to you.

Your woman's vulva becomes congested with blood, too. The labia majora swell and this swelling causes them to draw back, exposing the inner lips and the entrance to the vagina. The inner lips may also swell and change color to a darker pink; the clitoris may also swell and stiffen.

Another noticeable effect of sexual excitement in a woman's body is the secretion of lubricant by glands in the walls of the vagina. This prepares the vagina for the insertion of your erect penis.

When she is first aroused, your woman's nipples will usually stiffen, and her breasts may swell. The breasts of some young women grow by as much as a quarter when they are fully excited, simply because of the blood that rushes into them and expands them.

Later, as her excitement increases, your woman may develop what Masters and Johnson called the *sex flush*—a redness of the skin on the chest and face. This redness lasts through the excitement phase and the "plateau" phase that precedes orgasm, but quickly disappears once orgasm has been achieved—in much the same way that your erection instantly dies away once you have climaxed.

Your woman's vagina will relax and deepen, to give that mighty erection of yours plenty of room. Her womb will also rise so that the head of your penis is given adequate accommodation in the upper reaches of her body.

As you start having intercourse, and you enter the plateau phase that will eventually lead you up the mountain toward a climax, your woman's clitoris will withdraw under its hood of skin and remain retracted until she has an orgasm. Her heartbeat will increase dramatically and she will breathe up to thirty to forty times a minute.

The first feelings of orgasm occur in the lower third of the vagina and then quickly spread through the network of involuntary muscle to the remaining two-thirds. It is interesting to note that when a couple experience simultaneous orgasms during intercourse, the woman's vagina contracts every 0.8 seconds, and her first three or four contractions coincide exactly with the contractions that her partner experiences as he ejaculates sperm into her. So when we're talking about simultaneous orgasm, we're really talking simultaneous, down to the tenth of a second.

The contractile waves rapidly reach your woman's womb, and although the contractions of the womb are slower and not as regular as those of the vagina, they can give her the sensation that "the earth moved."

Her anal muscles will also contract involuntarily, which is why anal stimulation can add so much to her pleasure as she approaches her climax. Her urethral muscles go through the same spasm, which is why some women occasionally squirt out a little urine during their orgasm. This is quite normal, and some women do it on purpose in order to stimulate their lovers even more.

During orgasm your woman's nipples will remain erect, although it is a mistake to take nipple erection as an infallible sign that your woman has or has not reached an orgasm. Some women's nipples remain comparatively soft during their orgasm; others stiffen up to a half-inch even though they are nowhere near to reaching a climax.

Unlike you, your woman can experience a second or a third or a fourth orgasm directly after her first. Provided she keeps up the same level of stimulation, either by masturbating or by taking advantage of the fact that your penis has not fully flopped away, she can attain that state that Masters and Johnson called *status orgasmus*, in which she can go on experiencing orgasms for up to a minute, occasionally longer. It is probably easier for a man to rouse his woman into *status orgasmus* by masturbating her or licking her clitoris, because when she begins to climax he can maintain the same level of arousal for as long as she can take it, without interruption.

Theoretically, a woman can remain in *status orgasmus* almost indefinitely, but in practice other factors usually intervene. The woman may tire, her lover may stop stimulating her, or she may lose mental concentration. *Status orgasmus* is more often achieved during masturbation than during intercourse, since a woman can concentrate entirely on her own pleasure.

Immediately prior to orgasm, your woman's vagina will become very juicy with lubricant, but as I mentioned earlier, women do not ejaculate in the same way that men do. This is in spite of all those erotic tales such as *The Adventures of a Gentleman in Search of Pleasure*, written in 1880, whose author declared after describing his hundredth bout of intercourse, "When she rose off me, the sperm dropped from her salacious slit in large gouts upon me, attesting the bountiful measure with which nature had endowed both of us with the elixir of life." Or this, written in 1985, over a century later, in *Lovebirds* magazine, "I pushed my fingers all the way in and she gasped and heaved, and I felt her juices pour around my fingers. Before long her juices were really flowing and then she climaxed."

After orgasm the sexual flush fades, the nipples gradually soften, and the vulva loses its swelling. A woman's refractory period, however, is usually much shorter than a man's, and even if she has dropped below the plateau level of excitement, she can usually be brought back to it relatively quickly.

How can you take advantage of what you know about your woman's body and about the gradually-rising profile of her sexual excitement? How can you use your knowledge to improve your sexual skill and really drive her wild in bed?

- *Indulge* in as much imaginative foreplay as you can dream up, for as long as you like or as long as you can. Caress and fondle her breasts and her nipples, and don't forget other nervously sensitive areas such as the back, the sides of the body just above the hips, the insides of the thighs, the buttocks. Think of the areas on your own body where you enjoy being stroked, not necessarily sexually. The fact that you're now in a sexual situation will transform ordinary nervous stimulation into erotic stimulation. Don't be afraid to kiss your woman—mouth, eyes, nose, shoulders, breasts, everywhere. I am al-

ways surprised when women complain that
their lovers ignore their breasts. Masters
and Johnson found that three women in
their study group of more than 380 women
were capable of reaching orgasm simply
by fondling their own breasts; there is a
strong connection between breast-feeding
and sexual desire. A small percentage of
women can experience orgasms when they
are breast-feeding their babies. You can
take advantage of the same erotic reaction
by gently sucking your woman's nipples,
drumming them with the tip of your tongue
against the roof of your mouth, and at the
same time manipulating her breasts.

Show her that she turns you on, too, and
encourage her to react to your excitement.
Many men are so worried about their sexual technique and about their woman's
orgasm that they completely forget about
their own pleasure. Always remember that
pleasure is infectious. If you're enjoying
yourself, that's half the battle. And never
be afraid to tell her or show her how you
like to be aroused. She's not psychic, and
if she has enough feeling for you to want
to go to bed with you, she has enough
feeling to want to please you the best way
she can. Press your stiffened penis against
her body. Caress her breasts and nipples
with it. Show her that you're aroused.
Here's George, 27, from Seattle: "I guess
you could say that I was pretty backward
in coming forward when it came to sex. I
lost my cherry when I was 16, but up until
I was 25 you couldn't say that my love life

was anything to write home about. One of the troubles was that I always found it difficult to express myself to girls. I didn't know how to ask them out, I didn't know how to get them into bed, and even when I'd managed to inveigle a young lady into the sack, I didn't know how to show her what I felt. Every time I had sex it was just a lot of necking, followed by a whole lot of tossing and turning and rolling around the bed, followed by a quick fuck, and that was it. I kept asking myself, you know, is this it? Is this all there is to the much vaunted act of sex? Well, let me tell you, all this changed when I met Carole. We met at a disco downtown, and I couldn't take my eyes off her, I absolutely couldn't. She has curly blond hair and a beautiful face with bright blue eyes, and absolutely the biggest breasts I think I've ever seen. Her previous boyfriend kept telling her she ought to try for the *Playboy* centerfold, but she wouldn't, you know, she's too shy. I don't know how I managed it, but I just went straight up to her at this disco and said, 'How about a dance?' and she shrugged and said sure. Well, we danced, and I'm not a bad dancer, and we danced some more. Then I asked her out for a pizza, and she said sure to that too. I kept on asking and she kept on saying sure and in the end I took her back to my apartment. I played Dire Straits on the record player and dug out my special emergency bottle of red wine, and we danced some more, and then we started kissing. I took her into the bedroom and undressed her. She has a dynamite figure. Wide shoulders, narrow waist, and huge firm breasts with nipples as wide as cocktail coasters. We got on to the bed together and started kissing, but even though she was so pretty and so sexy I kept feeling the whole thing was just going to end the way it always did, you know, disappointing. But she said, 'What do I do to you? Do I turn you on?' And I said, 'Sure, you know, of course you turn me on.' But she said, 'Why aren't you showing it, then?' And this kind of caught me off guard. I said, 'I'm kissing you, aren't I?' And she said, 'Sure you're kissing me, but what about this?' And she took hold of my cock in her hand and rubbed it up and down two or three times. I was totally rigid anyway, I didn't need any extra turning on, but she said, 'Use it, it's fantastic,' and she wriggled down beside me, and kind of slipped herself down between my legs, and held up those huge big breasts of hers in both hands so that my cock was buried in between them. 'Come on,' she said, 'fuck my breasts. Don't you like my breasts?' And I said, 'Of course I like your breasts. You have fabulous breasts.' But she said, 'Go on, then, show me how much. Show me.' And so I took hold of my cock and massaged her breasts with it, and then she took over, and circled the head of my cock around and around her nipples until they began to rise, and my cock started to get real slippery with juice, and she smeared the juice over her nipples.

'There,' she said, 'now I can see that I'm turning you on.' She kissed the top of my cock and then she kind of rolled it around her face, kissing it now and then as if she was giving herself a massage. She even tickled the end of it with her eyelashes. That's when I reached down and started to stroke her between the legs, and her cunt was wet and she was more than ready to fuck. We dated for six months or so, went to bed whenever we could, but in the end she had to move to Los Angeles with her parents, and the whole thing kind of fizzled out. She taught me one thing, though, and that is you have to *show* girls the way you feel about them. That's what all the guys who are really successful with women do. They're never afraid to say, 'Wow, you're lovely,' or anything like that, and when they get into bed they never feel like they've got to be reserved or polite about being horny. Men like to know that they're making a girl feel excited. Girls like to know that they're making a man feel excited."

George's comments come slap-bang under the heading of respect—that same respect we were talking about right at the beginning of this book. Too often men fail to respect women's desires, and to understand that women need reassurance about the effect they're having on men. Taking charge of a sexual relationship in order to improve its technique and the mutual satisfaction of both participants doesn't mean concentrating on her fun at the expense of concentrating on your own. Before you know it, she'll start believing that you're not enjoying your relationship with her, and that you're making love to her simply because it's easier than not making love to her. Show her how happy you are that you're having sex with her, and show her in every way that you can think of. Remember the old Mae West line, "Is that a roll of dimes in your pants pocket, or are you pleased to see me?"

Stimulate her sexual organs as intensely as you can before actually penetrating her. You can do this with your tongue or your fingers or with your penis, although you will find it a great deal harder to hold yourself back if you try doing it with your penis. Penises and vaginas have a disconcerting habit of behaving like the two parts of a solenoid switch—turn them on and one flies irresistibly into the other. We've already talked about ways of arousing the clitoris by gently flicking or strumming it. Sometimes a little intermittent squeezing on either side of the clitoral hood can be arousing: what you're doing is applying indirect pressure to the buried part of the clitoris. The tongue is far more sensitive than the fingers, and far more controllable. You can vary the pressure of flicking on the clitoris with your tongue by infinitesimal degrees, from a strong cat-lapping to the faintest of tip-touches. You also have the added options of kissing and sucking your woman's vulva, and pushing your stiffened tongue into her vagina. More about oral sex in a later chapter, but here's Jim, a 23-year-old engineer from San Antonio, talking about his initiation into cunnilingus: "What I learned about sex I learned from my friends, and from magazines, and what was written on lockerroom walls. The groups of guys that I grew up with were real macho, football players and stock-car drivers and stuff like that. They treated girls like—you know, girls were to be fucked, and that was what it was all about. Well, I was just the same as they were. Our idea of a good time was a lot of drinking, a lot of drag racing around the block, and then taking a girl out someplace quiet and fucking her. Not much finesse in that, was there? I didn't even know that girls could have a climax until I was 19 or 20, and even when I found out I didn't much care. Then I went to Corpus Christi to stay with my cousin for a couple of weeks, and while I was there I got to meet the folks who lived next door. They had a daughter, Helen, and she was about four years older than me. Red hair, pretty face, real cute. Anyway, to cut a long story short I took her out a couple of times, and the second time we went back to her parents' house when they were away, and we played a few records, and then she asked me up to see her bedroom. I guess we both knew what was going to happen. We started kissing and taking each other's clothes off. She was really great when she was naked. She had very white skin and her pubic hair was just as red as the hair on top of her head. We lay on this Indian rug on the floor and fooled around for a while and then I got on top of her and was just about to fuck her when she cupped her hand over her snatch and said, 'I'm not ready yet.' I didn't know what in hell she was talking about. I said, 'What do you mean, you're not ready yet?' And so she said, 'You haven't done anything, you haven't turned me on at all.' That was a bummer; I didn't even know what to say. I felt like a stupid kid who didn't know anything at all. But Helen said, 'You can kiss me if you want to.' So I kissed her on the lips, and we did some French kissing and stuff, and then she said, 'Kiss me lower,' so I kissed her neck. Then she said, 'Lower,' and I thought, 'I get it, this is it, she wants me to kiss her tits.' So I kissed her tits. But then she said, 'Lower,' and so I kissed her stomach. But she still said 'Lower,' and there I was staring straight at her bush of bright red hair and her bright pink cunt lips pouting up at me, and I'd never done anything like that before, you know, wh-a-a-at? Kiss a girl's cunt? About the only thing I'd ever kissed that wasn't lips was a long neck with the cap off. But I bent down and I kissed her, thinking, you know, one kiss and that's it, but she ran her hands right into my hair, and clutched it tight, and said, 'Go on, kiss me again,' and so I kissed her again, and this time I could taste the taste of cunt, and it was weird in a way but it turned me on. She said, 'Lick me,' and so I licked her, and then I licked her again without being told, and then again, and in the end I was lying there between her legs holding her cunt lips open with my fingers and I was licking her all the way down from her clitoris right into her hole, and she was lying back on the rug and her thighs were shifting up and down, and she was moaning and mmm-ing and saying 'more, more,' all of the time. My whole face was covered in cunt juice, but when I finally came up to fuck her properly, she kissed me over and over, and then she licked her own juice off my face. I was shocked. I don't often admit it, you know, being shocked. But I think I grew up that day. I suddenly realized that there was a whole lot more to sex than just ramming your pecker into a girl's cunt and jumping up and down until it was over. I don't know if Helen came or not. But she was panting and shouting and she must have had a good time even if she didn't come. I guess I should have asked her but I didn't have the nerve. She seemed to know so much more about it than I did. But the next time I went out with a girl, I went down on her the same way Helen had showed me, and the results were pretty good. I wasn't an expert or anything, but the girl thought that just doing it was really sophisticated."

Penetrate her slowly and easily, after making sure that her vagina is well lubricated. Nothing is as awkward as trying to thrust your erection into a dry vagina. It causes discomfort both to you and your lady, and also shows that you're being too hasty. There may be times when you need a little extra lubrication; if you do, a quick slathering with saliva is usually sufficient; otherwise you can use KY jelly or any brand of neutral lubricant. Take your time sliding yourself in. Tease her a little, push your penis in a little way and then withdraw it again. Build up the erotic tension even more until she is virtually demanding you thrust it in. The sense of excitement and relief when you actually push yourself fully into her will be more than worth waiting for.

As you penetrate her, you should be able to feel the relaxed, accommodating condition of her vagina. She is in the early stages of excitement, her body "wants" you and is doing everything it can to make the admission of your penis easier and more alluring. Her womb will have risen in order to make room for the head of your penis, and unless you adopt a sexual position that pushes the cervix down again (such as lifting her legs right up so that her knees are almost next to her ears, and thrusting your penis vertically downward into her vagina) neither of you will be able to feel your penis rubbing against it.

Caress her continuously during lovemaking. Your sexual organs should not be your only point of contact. You will be able to read her body language as she becomes more and more excited. You will be able to feel her nipples erecting. You may even be able to feel her breasts swelling. You will certainly be able to sense her quickening heart rate and hear her breathing speeding up. All of these signs will guide you as you make love, and enable you to judge whether you ought to slow your thrusting a little because she hasn't yet reached a sufficient state of arousal for you to be able to think about climaxing, or whether you ought to speed up a little because she's very close to the first stages of orgasm and you're not. Whatever you do during love-making, don't rush it. You have all the time in the world (unless you're making out in a slowly ascending office elevator) and you ought to enjoy what you're doing, both of you, to the very last drop.

This is Samantha, aged 31, the wife of a naval officer from San Diego. "I was first married when I was 19. The marriage lasted four years, and then we broke up. I was living in Omaha, Nebraska, at the time, and I decided to come out to California and look for a new life. Almost the first person I met was Danny. He took me out, showed me the sights, and I suppose you could say that he swept me off my feet. We dated for about two weeks and then he took me to the Rancho Bernardo Inn for dinner, a fantastically romantic dinner, and afterward he said that he'd booked a room, and if I wanted to, we could spend the night. If I wanted to! He had to be kidding. We went to our room after dinner and he had ordered a bottle of pink champagne. I think we managed to drink half a glass before we were both undressed and lying on top of the bed and kissing each other frantically, like two people who hadn't been allowed to kiss for a year. Danny was marvelous, very gentle and affectionate; he stroked my body like he was playing a musical instrument, can you understand that? And all my nerves tingled. He kissed my nipples, kissed my shoulders, and kissed me—well, just every place you can think of. You think I'm being shy? Well, maybe I am. But yes, he kissed me there too. What I always remember, though, is the way that he kept on kissing me and stroking me when we were making love, which was something my first husband had never done, not so beautifully anyway. He stroked my breasts and held me like I was something exciting and precious. That was the feeling he gave me, that I was *valuable* to him, that he wanted to look after me and take care of me no matter what. When we started getting really excited, really turned on, he stroked and fondled all around my vagina and all around my bottom, and took hold of my hand and said, 'Feel this—this is where we join. This is where you and me are one person.' Even though I was embarrassed, I let him guide my fingers right between our legs, and I could feel his penis sliding in and out of me; I could feel that he was actually inside me. I stroked his balls and I ran my fingers all the way round his penis, and he was running his fingers around there, too, so that we were both caressing each other right where we joined, and the feeling was marvelous. He slid one finger up inside me alongside his penis, and I slid a finger up there, too, right next to his, so that we could both feel what it was like inside my vagina while we were making love. Nobody had ever touched me like that before; nobody had ever explored me like that. Danny was teaching me things without even saying a word. He wasn't afraid of sex, and wasn't afraid of our bodies. Yet he was completely respectful: that was what you were talking about, wasn't it, respect?"

Nobody knows all there is to know about sex, simply because each act of lovemaking is a new and different experience, even between people who have been living together for more years than they care to count. That is why Danny's exploratory caressing was so important, both for him and for Samantha. It conveyed Danny's intense interest in Samantha's body, but also enabled both of them to visualize the very place where Danny's flesh bonded with Samantha's flesh, and to revel in the closeness and the sheer erotic pleasure of that bonding. It enabled them to learn about each other's bodies and each other's feelings, and most of all it was a sharing of physical secrets, a mutual offering to each other of their most intimate parts.

Caressing your woman during sex is essential. It shows that you are interested in sharing your feelings with her: you are not simply using her body to relieve your sexual tensions. You will also find that your caresses enable you to sense how excited your woman is becoming, to feel the rising of her nipples, the tensing of her muscles, the acceleration of her pulse rate. A fundamental part of being a good lover is using your fingers as well as your penis, and giving your woman the maximum amount of stimulation you can, not just during foreplay but all the way through the act of love.

Sex instruction books of the 1960s and 1970s used to talk with great seriousness about the erogenous zones. These were supposed to be designated areas on the human body that were especially sensitive to erotic stimulation. My experience is that it is quite pointless to worry about locating and stimulating particular areas of your woman's body. Caress her warmly and arousingly all over; your instincts will lead you to the places where she enjoys being fondled the most. You don't have to worry about locating Spot A or Spot B. If she's a human being and not an alien from another galaxy, she'll enjoy you titillating her mouth, her ears, her breasts, her vagina, and her anus, and everywhere else besides. The feet are very sensitive: you ought to try playing footsy with her during intercourse. You'll be surprised how much it excites her.

Respond to the way in which her vagina changes shape during intercourse. As you take her up the plateau toward orgasm, you should be able to feel the deepest recesses of her vagina open wider while the muscles in the lower third of the vagina begin to tense up. You can change your thrusting action to suit the change in shape of her vagina, alternating shallow, playful thrusts that will stimulate the lower, tighter part, with deep powerful thrusts that will reach right into the wide-open posterior fornix. This combination of quick, light stimulation of the orgasmic platform with forceful pushes that can help to initiate muscular spasms in the uterus will give her feelings a deeply pleasurable dimension and help her to attain an orgasm much more quickly than the usual monotonous in-and-out. You can actually take your penis right out of her vagina when you are giving her the lighter, more titillating thrusts; thus, when you reinsert the head of your penis, you will be tugging gently at her labia minora and adding to the indirect stimulation that your act of intercourse is already giving to her clitoris. As her orgasm begins to approach, you will feel the tension in her vaginal muscles gripping fiercely the shaft of your penis. Her entire body will tighten, her face will clench into an expression that looks almost as if she is in pain, and she will cling to you tightly, forcing her pubic bone against yours to increase the stimulating pressure on her clitoris and also to make sure that you ejaculate right up inside her. If you too are close to a climax, you will feel the same high tension and the same urge to push yourself closer and closer, as deep into her body as possible. Now your knowledde of what is happening inside your woman's body really comes into play. You should be able to sense how close she is to orgasm by the rapidity of her breathing, by the sexual flush of her skin, by the erection of her nipples, and by the viselike tightness of her muscles. You may even begin to feel the first muscular ripples of the vaginal barrel, the first twitches of an imminent climax.

This is when you have to *time* yourself carefully, especially if you want to enjoy your orgasms simultaneously. While simultaneous orgasm is a highly exciting and desirable experience, it is not an essential for happy and satisfying sex. Most couples do not have simultaneous orgasms most of the time, and still lead red-hot sex lives. Simultaneous orgasm is just one of those things that happens when the mood is right, when you both happen to be equally stimulated at almost the same moment, and when your minds and bodies are working together in particularly close harmony. It is possible, however, to increase the *likelihood* of simultaneous orgasm, and at the least to reduce the gap between your climax and hers so that you both reach the peak of sexual excitement within seconds of each other. Timing yourself well requires patience, expertise, and experience. You will find it difficult to begin with, but if you make sure that you are keenly alert to the physical changes that are taking place in your woman's body, if you listen to her body language, you should be able to slow yourself down or speed yourself up accordingly.

A man occasionally suffers from premature ejaculation, especially when he is young. This means that he becomes so sexually aroused during lovemaking that he shoots out his semen long before his woman is ready for him . . . leaving *him* with a flaccid penis that wouldn't push a hole in an unbaked pizza, and *her* with a vagina full of longing and no way of relieving it. It *is* possible for a man to delay his climax by turning his mind to matters apart from sex, like the political situation in the Philippines, or whether mass transit is economically viable in the state of Michigan, but this kind of turning-your-mind-off technique is both unreliable and no fun at all. After all, you're in bed with this lady to have sex, not to start thinking about elections and railroad services.

Premature ejaculation, like many other psychosexual problems, is largely a matter of habit. In other words, it's self-perpetuating. The more a man believes that he's going to ejaculate too soon, the likelier he is to do it. The best way to break such a habit is to use a physical technique, like the tried-and-trusted Masters and Johnson grip.

Premature ejaculators should enlist the help of their loved ones in order to make this technique work effectively. It's very simple and it works like this: whenever a man feels that he is approaching a premature climax, he should withdraw his penis from his woman's vagina (that's if intercourse has actually begun—otherwise, all he has to do is tell her that he's close to coming). His woman then grasps the shaft of his penis with the ball of her thumb on the frenum, that little web of skin just below the urethral opening, and presses hard. This squeeze can be repeated as often as necessary, right up to (and past) the moment when the woman has reached an orgasm. The happy result, seven times out of ten, is that once a man has realized that he is capable of delaying his climax, he can do it without resorting to the squeeze.

Temporary impotence is a little more difficult to overcome, but is caused by similar physical and psychological factors: stress, tiredness, the effects of alcohol, and again, the very fear of it happening.

Whenever you are suffering from any kind of sexual problem, and particularly when you are having trouble producing and sustaining an erection, tell the woman in your life what's going wrong. If you don't, she's going to begin to feel resentful, frustrated, and suspicious. You have to teach her that a few failures on your part to get a viable hard-on are completely normal in today's stressful society, and that it happens to most men at one time or another. *It does not mean that anything is physically wrong with you.* Nor does it mean that you no longer love her, that she no longer arouses you, or that you have your eye on another woman. It simply means that all kinds of external factors have combined to make it difficult for you to be erotically stimulated, no matter how much you may *want* to be erotically stimulated.

The only way you can break the self-perpetuating cycle (impotence causes fear of impotence, which in turn causes impotence) is by continuing your sexual relationship quietly and without tension, using oral and masturbatory techniques, and satisfying each other the best way you can. Your erections will return naturally; just as long as your woman knows that you haven't "gone off her." And, quite often, a short period without intercourse can develop your other sexual techniques to a very refined pitch.

The causes and cures of male sexual problems are rarely taught to women with any clarity, so if you're having any difficulties yourself, it's more than likely going to be your responsibility to tell her what's gone wrong and how you're going to get over it. If you feel it will help, show her this book. She may not agree with all of the sexual opinions that I've expressed, but she can't deny the simple effectiveness of well-tried techniques and the benefits of mutual respect and understanding. Just as you're making an effort to understand her sexual needs, so she should make an equal effort to understand yours.

Here's Roger, 26, a young advertising executive from Los Angeles: "I'd been chasing Gayle for months, trying to get her to go out with me. In the end she said yes, and of course I was absolutely delighted. She was very attractive, long dark brown hair, dark eyes, slightly Slavic looking, terrific figure. I took her out to the theater, then we had a late dinner and went dancing. About one o'clock in the morning I took her back to my apartment in Venice. We went at each other like tigers, kissing, biting, clawing, all the rest of it, and I took her through to the bedroom and took off her dress. She unbuttoned my shirt, unbuckled my belt, and reached into my pants and took hold of my cock. I was hard as a billy club. She kissed me, and tugged my cock a couple of times, and do you know what happened? I came in her hand. I shot sperm all over her arm, and thought: This is it, damn it, it's all over and it hasn't even begun. Of course I was utterly shaken, and I felt about as virile as a 13-year-old kid. But I said, 'As long as you're here, we might as well have a drink', and we sat on the sofa naked and shared a bottle of good red wine. I said, 'That can happen sometimes, coming too quick. It means that a guy is nervous and overexcited and that maybe he wants to make love to you just a little too much. I hope you can take it as a compliment and not as an insult.' I didn't know then about the Masters and Johnson squeeze, otherwise I would have told her about that too. But I managed to persuade her that what had happened was normal, that it didn't mean anything, and I think the light kind of half dawned, because she leaned forward on the sofa and she took hold of my cock and started to rub it up and down until it stiffened up again. Then without a word she climbed on top of me and guided my cock up between her legs. Her hair hung down and covered my face—I'll always remember that—and her breasts kept swinging so that her nipples grazed my chest.

She went up and down on me real slow, and we made love like that for more than ten minutes until she was gasping and sweating and panting, and we were gripping onto each other like we were afraid we were going to fall off the world. We had a climax together, and that was the first time I'd ever experienced that. Obviously I didn't shoot as much sperm as I had the first time, but it was still a good ball-gripping climax, if you'll excuse the expression, and we both ended up satisfied. And do you know what she said to me? 'Next time, I'll make sure that you come first, then we'll have some wine and fool around a little and then we'll get down to the real nitty-gritty.' That was the most uplifting, human thing she could have said. And it worked, too, because the next time I didn't shoot off right away, I kept my climax back right till the last moment. We had a good sexual relationship that lasted for seven or eight months. After that we just drifted apart. But I never suffered from a hairtrigger climax again. Gayle had helped me to get over it completely."

Roger should take a little more credit himself for having plucked up the courage to discuss his predicament with Gayle and make sure that she understood what had happened. By taking the trouble to come clean about it, he had reassured her that everything was sexually okay between them, and the result was that he managed to resurrect his erection and give her all the satisfaction that she demanded.

Even when you are not having trouble with impotence or premature ejaculation, timing yourself to drive your woman the wildest possible can still be a problem. Men and women become sexually aroused at a different pace, and since the physical indications of *her* approaching orgasm are usually more obvious than *yours*, it is much easier for you to be able to time your climax. It's rather like an arcade video game that requires a bomber pilot (you) to drop your bomb into the crater of a volcano (her) at the instant the volcano erupts.

You can substantially improve your mental and physical control over your climax by practicing what I call the E-Technique—E standing for Ejaculation. This is one sexual technique you can practice by yourself that will have directly beneficial effects on your lovemaking.

Let's see how it works.

6.
The E-Technique—How to Fine-Tune Your Climax

I talked earlier about the feasibility of reaching a climax without any physical stimulus—in other words, how you can learn to ejaculate without intercourse and without masturbating in the conventional sense.

The importance of trying to reach a climax without physical stimulus is that it teaches you to fine-tune your mental control over your penis. You can, literally, *think* yourself into having a climax.

In much the same way that women are recommended by sex therapists to pleasure themselves by finding a warm, comfortable place to masturbate without any possibility of being disturbed, you should do the same if you want to advance your sexual proficiency with the E-Technique. Take a night off from whatever you do at night—hanging around singles bars, boogying the night away at the local disco, making time with three women at once, or staring out of the window—and prepare yourself for a couple of hours of complete sexual concentration.

Take a shower, play some music, drink a glass of wine. If you have sex magazines or erotic videos, take a look at them to put you in the mood. When you're feeling really relaxed, however, take yourself to bed, naked, and lie in complete darkness. Think of the women to whom you'd like to make love. Think of the times when you have made love and how erotic it was. This is going to be a time for sexual thought and nothing else, so dismiss any anxieties that have been left over from a hard day at the office. This is *your* time, *your* moment, when you're going to start improving your control over your body.

You should have some contact with your penis. Hold it in one hand with your finger and thumb around the glans. Lightly pressing the frenum with the tip of your index finger might give you extra contact with the subtle changes in hardness and sensitivity that are going to be taking place in it.

Now, think of your favorite erotic fantasy. Think yourself *into* it, almost as if you can imagine that you're actually there. Have no inhibitions whatever about it, because the E-Technique is concerned not only with controlling your physical responses but controlling your mental responses as well, and there will be times when you're making love that you will need to summon up the strongest erotic fantasy you can think of in order to speed up your ejaculation. So to begin with, try to conjure up the most vivid erotic images you can, and see how quickly you can arouse yourself into a full erection. But remember, the hand that grasps your penis should remain still—no rubbing, no squeezing, or other stimulation. This time when you climax, you're going to do it by mental power alone.

Leon, a 30-year-old petroleum engineer from Dallas, described to me his own personal fantasy, the one he used when he first tried the E-Technique: "I first had this fantasy when I was about 20 or 21, and I was working on an offshore rig in the Gulf; two months without seeing a woman and that was hard going, in every sense of the word. I began to build up this fantasy about a girls' college, a college where parents sent girls who were really highly sexed, girls who wanted to be high-class hookers and hostesses and call girls, girls who wanted to use their bodies to make a living. So in my fantasy was this girls' college, girls only, especially made to teach girls how to make love. And right from their first day these girls weren't allowed to wear any clothes at all, except stockings and garter belts if they wanted to, and stiletto-heeled shoes, even when they were in class. And I used to picture this first class, with all these naked girls sitting at their desks, all of them pretty, of course, 16 or 17 years old, with long hair and big breasts, every one of them gorgeous, and in comes the teacher. She's a statuesque brunette, five-ten, with enormous breasts, all she's wearing is stockings and high heels, and what she does is sit on a chair in front of the class and open up her pussy with her fingers and say, 'The first thing I want you to do is feel what a woman's pussy is like.' All the class has to go forward one by one and push their fingers up the teacher's pussy. Then the teacher shows them how to masturbate, and they all sit at their desks masturbating while the teacher walks around and watches them. And so it goes on. It's kind of an endless fantasy, I can think up all kinds of variations when I'm really feeling horny, like a parents' evening when the parents come around to watch their daughters giving demonstrations of fucking on the school stage, and brothers and sisters are invited to join in, and maybe there's one girl who specializes in making it with animals, and she gives a demonstration of fellating this Great Dane, or having intercourse with a pony. I mean, when you talk about a fantasy in the cold light of day, it sounds really extreme, but when you're really turned on, and your mind is blazing away at white heat, a fantasy is a fantasy, and you can imagine anything you like and all it does is turn you on. Afterwards it fades, and you don't think about it again, so where's the harm?"

Believe it or not, Leon's fantasy was comparatively mild. During the course of preparing this chapter, I talked to more than fifty men about their erotic fantasies, and most of them were far more extreme. But, as Leon pointed out, a fantasy is only a fantasy. It's nothing more than imagination, a mental stimulus to increase the body's pleasure, and when the body has been satisfied, the fantasy disappears. Fantasy plays a vital part in exciting sexual relationships, both for men and for women, and you should never be embarrassed or ashamed about your "dirtier" erotic thoughts. Sometimes you may want to play them out for real with your sexual partner, but more often than not you will find that they are far more effective if they remain fantasies, unhampered by reality, unbounded by anything except your erotic tastes and your erotic demands.

"I used to fantasize about making love to a pregnant woman," said James, 33, from Gary, Indiana. "I saw some photographs in a sex magazine once of a heavily pregnant woman, and the idea of climbing on top of that rounded stomach and pushing my cock into her, right next to her baby, for some reason that really turned me on. There was one picture in which she was holding her cunt open, and her cunt was very swollen and red and glistening, but very tight too, and that's just one of those sexual images that's stuck in my mind."

Ben, who's 34 and comes from Betteravia, California, has fantasized for years about being tied up and disciplined by a "dominatrix." "She has me handcuffed in an upstairs bedroom, naked, and sometimes she keeps me there for days on end without coming up to see me. When she does, she's always dressed in a black leather basque and black leather thigh boots, with her breasts bulging out of the top of the basque and her sex completely exposed. She has blond hair, cut very short, and a very severe-looking face, but beautiful too. She mocks me and slaps my face. Sometimes she kneels between my legs and strokes my cock until I'm just about to climax, and then she takes her hand away. It's all teasing and taunting. Sometimes she whips me, lashing my shoulders and my chest and my legs, and whenever she whips me I always get a tremendous erection, even though it hurts so much. She draws blood. Then she stands in front of me and holds her pussy open and urinates all over my cuts so that they sting really fiercely. That was something I read in a Harold Robbins novel. I guess it's pretty crude, but that's what fantasies are, aren't they? A way of being crude without upsetting anybody, and let's face it, everybody has crude ideas at one time or another, right?"

The reason I've quoted these fantasies is to show you that when you're practicing the E-Technique, anything that you can possibly imagine is permissible. The stronger and more erotic the mental pictures you can conjure up, the better, because you're attempting a sexual feat that isn't at all easy; to reach a climax without any physical stimulation at all. Your mind is in sole control of your state of arousal, and if your mind wavers or wanders or loses its sense of direction, your erection will inevitably fade and you'll have to start turning yourself on all over again. So, your mind has to conjure up vivid and extreme images, images that are going to grab you by the testicles and not let go.

Although your imagination is very much in the driver's seat, you can use your internal muscles to assist you in reaching a climax. With care, you should be able to feel the spasms that convey semen to the urethral bulb, all ready for ejaculation. With care, you should be able to feel the first slight twitchings that will eventually lead to a climax.

You will find that you can shift your erotic attention from the area of your urethral bulb at the base of your penis right up to the head of the penis, and back again, at will. As your fantasies take hold, and the muscles in your perineal region begin to clench, you will want to concentrate on your glans, the most sensitive area, because it is friction on this part that eventually brings you to ejaculate.

The E-Technique is not simple to acquire. It takes concentration and practice, and you may try it seven or eight times before you are able to ejaculate without any physical stimulation at all. You will find it mentally and physically exhausting, even though you've been doing nothing more than lying in bed with one hand around your cock, thinking erotic thoughts. It is obviously more difficult to achieve a nonstimulated climax when you're having regular sex than it is when you're "resting" between affairs, but married men can try their hand at it during their wife's period or when they're away from home on a business trip. There's nothing shameful or sinful or disloyal about it—especially since its prime purpose is to improve your sexual control with the woman you want the most.

Some men find that they can attain an E-Technique climax much more readily when they're lying on their backs. Others prefer to lie sideways, with their legs slightly drawn up, so that the pressure of their thighs stimulates their genital region. A few gentle squeezes with the hand that clasps your penis are permissible: in fact, you may find it extremely difficult to resist masturbating in the normal way. But the less you can touch your penis, the better. You're attempting to control your physical responses from the inside of your mind, and once you have achieved even a small degree of success you will find that you are a far more skillful and

competent lover. You will find that you can delay your climax or speed it up simply by select-
ing the right fantasy, the right degree of concentration, and by complementing that mental
concentration with a high degree of awareness
of what is happening inside your own genitals.

When you are actually making love, of course,
your penis will be subject to unremitting stimulation, and so you will find that you do not
need the same intense level of concentration in
order to climax as when you are practicing the
E-Technique on your own. You will, in fact,
have greater control over your sexual responses
than you really need; but that extra 10 percent
of physical and mental control will add enormously to your sense of sexual confidence.

Confidence breeds confidence just as fear
breeds fear, and if you convey a feeling of being
sexually in charge, your woman will respond to
it enthusiastically. Although she expects satisfaction on equal terms, and although she expects to participate equally in your lovemaking,
she will still be stimulated by your display of
virility and sexual self-possession and by the
feeling of being "taken." Sounds old-fashioned,
I know, but there are some biological urges
that never change, regardless of sexual politics.
If you are eager and highly aroused and a skillful lover, you will be showing her that you care
about her and that you find her sexually irresistible—who wouldn't be stimulated by that?

As I have said, it may take seven or eight
attempts before you are able to use the E-
Technique to ejaculate spontaneously. But it
can be done, and when it happens, it will give
you a tremendous sense of achievement.

The intensity of an E-Technique ejaculation is almost always stunning—far more intense than anything you will have experienced through masturbation or normal sexual intercourse. Jed, 32, from San Diego, said, "It took me nine or ten tries to reach a climax with the E-Technique. After about the fifth try, I began to believe that it wasn't even possible, that it was nothing more than one of those useless gimmicks with an initial letter in front of it, like an H-Diet or a X-Ercise. But eventually I managed to fix on a fantasy that really turned me on like you wouldn't believe. I thought about having sex in the woods in the summer in the pouring rain, crawling through the mud with this beautiful girl who's completely naked, her hair all wet and her body all smeared with mud, and we lie down in the leaves and we fuck like animals. It was incredible. Suddenly I could almost imagine that I was there. I actually imagined what it would feel like, pushing myself in and out of her, and all the time she's twisting and moaning and digging her nails in me. I swear that I could almost feel her. I could almost see her gripping her own breasts, and her nipples standing out; and her hair is all spread out in the mud and the leaves but she doesn't care, all she cares about is being fucked. Then suddenly I got this feeling down in the root of my cock, and I thought, I'm coming. It was like a convulsion, you know, much stronger than anything I've ever felt before, it was like I could feel all of my tubes twitching. The head of my cock felt like it was going to explode, I can't even describe what it felt like. For one second I lost my concentration, but then I thought about climaxing up inside this girl's body, and the sperm came shooting up my cock like an express train, and I had the kind of climax you read about in porno stories. You know, a climax that totally shook me, and I just went on shooting and shooting and shooting. I don't suppose I actually ejaculated any more than normal, but the convulsions were so strong, I ended up exhausted, panting, but it was such an incredible feeling to think that I'd actually brought myself off not by jerking off, not by any artificial methods at all, but simply by *thinking* myself into a climax. I could understand then the relationships between what goes on in your mind and what happens when you make love."

Had his experience of the E-Technique improved Jed's lovemaking? "Slowly, yes. I don't believe that you can change anything overnight: your weight, your golf swing, your reading ability. You have to work at it. But the next time I made love to my girlfriend, Esther, I used my imagination a whole lot more, and I was more conscious about the feelings inside my own body. I found that after a while I was able to relate the responses I was getting from her with my own responses. We still haven't managed to climax simultaneously—I guess that's my ultimate goal—but we always climax pretty close together, and Esther has commented herself that we seem to have found a new sexual closeness."

If you have tried the E-Technique as many as a dozen times and still find that you are unable to ejaculate without some external stimulus, then there is no harm in allowing yourself some minimal extra manipulation. One volunteer found it made all the difference if he tugged downward on his penis while he was nearing a climax; another discovered that he could trigger his ejaculation by inserting a single finger into his anus and gently pressing on the area of the prostate gland (that is, in a forward beckoning motion). Several others found that they could reach the brink of climax but never quite manage to get over it, so two or three masturbatory hand strokes were called for.

Added stimulations like these are not "cheating," and will not seriously affect the psychosexual training that the E-Technique will give you. However, you should only resort to them if it becomes apparent that you are not going to be able to reach a climax without them—and after fifteen minutes of concentrated erotic thought, you *will* feel an almost irresistible need to ejaculate.

Just make sure that you are happy in your own mind that you have done everything possible to attain a climax with the minimum of physical stimulation. It is an achievement in itself to bring yourself to the very edge of ejaculatory inevitability with no other form of arousal than your own fantasies. If you can't quite make the last hurdle—well, that's nothing to feel bad about. It takes a special kind of willpower and sexual concentration to be able to rouse yourself from having a soft penis to full ejaculation by imagination alone.

Several men who have tried the E-Technique have remarked that it distinctly improves the quality of their climax. Peter, 34, from Madison, Wisconsin, said, "I found that I was able to hold myself back much more easily. I could do it fast but best of all I could do it *slow*. When I did it slow, the feeling was always that much better for being held back. In fact, the longer I could hold it back, the more explosive it was when it actually happened. To tell you the truth, my sex life with Lena had started getting dull. We'd been married for thirteen years and after thirteen years you can get jaded. But when I started using the E-Technique, I suddenly got interested in Lena all over again, I suddenly thought, 'Hey this is not just a question of two people coupling for no reason at all except that they're married, this is two people making love and using their bodies to give each other pleasure and comfort and satisfaction.' Well, of course that wouldn't have happened if I hadn't been able to control myself very much more than I ever had before."

The E-Technique has its critics. Some therapists believe that it turns a man's erotic attention onto himself when he should be concentrating on his partner—and that this leads to "compartmentalized sex": two people having intercourse with each other but thinking of nothing but their own responses. Every man I know who has tried the E-Technique, however, reports the opposite: His newly improved ability to fine-tune his climax has made him much more interested in his woman's pleasure. In fact, several said they now took considerable pride in being able to time their ejaculations to coincide almost exactly with their partner's orgasm.

None of them said that they found the E-Technique easy, but then few abilities that are easy to acquire are very effective.

Will the E-Technique infallibly enable you to experience simultaneous orgasm?

The answer is no—not that simultaneous orgasm is always necessary or desirable. However, the E-Technique can dramatically improve your chances of both experiencing orgasm during the moments when you are experiencing maximum sexual arousal—in other words within a few seconds of each other. There will be fewer occasions when one partner is left struggling to bring the other partner to an inevitable but long-delayed climax after he or she has "finished." Peter said, "In the bad old days, there used to be times when I was masturbating Lena to give her an orgasm ten or fifteen minutes after I'd climaxed—when all I really wanted to do was close my eyes and drop off to sleep."

At least he was dutiful enough to make sure that Lena reached an orgasm. Many men wouldn't have bothered. But lovemaking that is performed as a duty can quickly lead to resentment and to other psychosexual complications. The E-Technique goes a long way toward making sure that you delay or accelerate your climax so that the arousal gap between you and your woman is lessened sufficiently to take away any feeling that bringing her up to a climax is—dare I say it?—a chore.

Your sexual imagination is one of the greatest assets you have. Not only can you use it to practice the E-Technique, but you can share it with your bed partner in order to keep your sexual relationship at a highly erotic pitch. Later we'll see how you can introduce even your strongest sexual fantasies into your lovemaking—for your excitement and for her satisfaction.

At the moment, however, let's hear from Don, a 29-year-old architect from Racine, Wisconsin, on how he used his sexual fantasies to control his ejaculatory responses. Don was one of the most successful "guinea pigs" who tried the E-Technique and he reported that he was able to come to a nonmanipulatory climax on only the third occasion he tried it. "Mind you," he said, "my wife was staying with her mother in Indiana for the week, so I didn't have any other sexual outlet."

Don's principal erotic fantasy revolves around being a ringmaster at a kind of sexual circus. "I guess you might think it's childish. I've always liked circuses ever since I was a small boy. I always thought there was something vulgar and glittery and dirty about them. I wanted to be a lion tamer up until the time I was 10 or 11. You must think that being an architect is quite a comedown after that!"

Don had originally written to me because of difficulties with premature ejaculation. I recommended the E-Technique, and he tried it immediately, even though he admitted that he had considerable misgivings about a man of 29 being able to achieve a climax using little more than the power of his own imagination.

"I had a small whiskey to loosen myself up. Then I lay on the bed and switched off the lights, as per instructions, and held my cock loosely in my hand and waited. It's pretty hard to think erotic thoughts to order. The first couple of times I tried it, I kept getting mental interference from other parts of my brain, wondering whether I was going to have time to take the car around to the body shop the following morning and where was I going to eat tomorrow night.

"On the third occasion, though, I was more relaxed. Maybe I was more tired. Whatever, I found it easier to slip into my circus fantasy, and before I knew it my cock started to harden. It hardened and softened, hardened and softened, but in the end I was able to work myself up to a pitch when it came up hard and stayed hard.

"I always imagine that I'm the ringmaster, and that the stars of the circus are nude girls. Every one of them is ravishing, of course. They have plumed headdresses, just like those chorus girls you see in Vegas, and high-heel shoes, and some of them have glittery silver thongs, but otherwise they're completely naked. They have to keep smiling all the time, no matter what they're doing, and no matter what's being done to them.

"To begin with, the girls go through a normal circus routine, dancing and tumbling in front of the audience. Some of them do like a limbo dance in front of the audience, so that their vaginas are wide open and everybody can see. I always like to imagine that the audience is half shocked and half fascinated. Then we have the first act, which is a statuesque brunette—I always imagine she looks a little bit like Sophia Loren—she comes riding into the ring on the back of this huge dapple-gray horse. She's sitting up totally straight with a huge headdress of ostrich feathers. But it's only when she comes around for the second time that I crack my ringmaster's whip at her, and she starts to lift herself up and down on the horse's back, and then everybody can see for the first time that there's a girth right around the horse's middle, and this girth has a huge artificial cock fitted on to it so that every time the girl lifts herself up and down, the cock slides in and out of her vagina.

"I did what you suggested and 'slowed down' the action whenever I felt that I was getting too sexually excited. With this fantasy, all I had to do was imagine that the girl was sitting back down on the horse again, so that the artificial cock was no longer visible. It was still erotic, you know, but not so blatant. Then, when I wanted to intensify my sexual feeling, I imagined her lifting herself right up in the stirrups and riding slowly around the ring so that everybody could see this great thick shining rubber penis that was forcing her vagina wide open.

"Usually I imagine that she rides around and around until she has an orgasm. She sits on the horse digging her fingers into its mane and screaming with the pleasure of it.

"Then I have this fantasy about nude acrobats, men and women, all of them completely nude, with shaved heads and shaved bodies, and all covered with oil. Three men form a pyramid holding up a fourth man, and this man has a tremendous erection. One of the girls climbs up and sits on top of him with her legs wide apart so that his erection slides right up into her vagina, and everybody in the circus can see. All of these women acrobats are exquisitely beautiful, very haughty, very exotic. They wear gold earrings and some of them wear rings through their nipples.

"Anyhow, more and more men and women

climb onto this human pyramid, and each of them is joined in a sexual way. The first girl holds one man's erection in her mouth, and another man's erection in her hand. Each of these men is holding up another girl, one of them leaning his head back and supporting her between the legs with his open mouth while the other man has inserted one of his fingers up her bottom to keep her steady, and so it goes on. I guess you could say that it defies the laws of gravity and anatomy, maybe the laws of morality too, but I can build it up into a really powerful erotic fantasy.

"The fantasy that actually brought me up to a climax was a clown scene. My fantasy circus has a clown act in which these clowns in baggy pants and funny faces chase this naked girl around. They throw buckets of water over her and keep groping at her and nearly catching her, and so she goes to the chief clown, who has this white mysterious masked face and this silvery spangled costume, and she gets down on her hands and knees and begs him to call the clowns off. He opens up a seam in the front of his costume and takes out his cock, and demands that she goes down on him. Everybody in the whole circus watches in complete silence while this beautiful naked girl takes this masked man's cock between her lips and starts sucking him and licking him. Sometimes she takes him into her mouth right down to the seam of his costume so that you can't see his cock at all; it must be halfway down her throat. Then two of the other clowns, the ones they call the *augustes*, they take hold of the girl's bottom and thighs and they spread them wide apart so that the whole audience can see, and they start to finger-fuck her, two of them, both at the same time, and all the time she's sucking the masked clown's cock, and she starts trembling and shaking and her whole body starts jerking, and finally the white-faced clown is almost ready to climax.

"Now here again I can slow down the fantasy if I don't want to climax myself. I can imagine that the white-faced clown simply holds his cock tantalizingly in front of her face and won't let her suck it, and the other clowns stop finger-fucking her, and everything's held in suspense. By that time, I don't lose my sexual tension, but I can hold off a climax. Then I can imagine that the girl starts to run her tongue up and down his cock, and he climaxes all over her tongue; and she climaxes too because the other clowns thrust their fingers up her and bring her off."

Don found that he didn't fantasize in such intense detail when he was making love. Too much of his attention was fixed on the girl with whom he was having sex. But his practice with the E-Technique enabled him to conjure up certain key images that helped either to arouse him or to slow him down.

The E-Technique is not an exact scientific method of controlling the male climax. It is simply a way of training your mind and your body to work in accord. I would be interested to hear how other men respond to E-Technique training, particularly in the area of delaying premature ejaculation. I would also like to hear how women respond to men who have tried the technique. As one young wife told me, "Tom gives me feelings I never had before because he never used to last this long before. I'm all in favor."

7

From Opening Line to Opening Thighs . . . How to Get a Woman into Bed

I have unfairly supposed until now that you have a hotly passionate and highly willing wife or lover already waiting for you in the bedroom, her hair spread out across the pillow, her nipples already rising in anticipation, her silk stockings zizzing against each other, her lips moistened.

If so, you'd better put this book down and do what needs to be done. But if not—if you're away from home, in between lovers, or haven't yet found the woman of your hottest desires—well, there's some useful discussion we can have about that. There is no man in the whole wide world, no matter how successful he is with women, who couldn't use a little advice and criticism.

Today's status- and dress-conscious woman expects more out of your appearance and manner than ever before. Because of this, you will rarely get the women you want unless you are stylish and determined, and being stylish and determined isn't always as easy as it sounds.

Being stylish and determined does not mean strutting around with your shirt wide open, snapping your fingers at barkeeps, and generally coming on like a Macho Man. Apart from the excruciating antiquity of this kind of image and behavior, it will probably attract nobody these days but other men of a certain disposition, and while I have nothing against other men of a certain disposition, this book is called—well, you remember what it's called. It's about women.

Take a look at yourself in a full-length mirror, naked to begin with. Do you think you're good-looking? Do you think you're potentially good-looking but don't quite know how to go about grooming yourself? Are you in reasonable physical shape? Be critical of yourself but also be optimistic. After all, Woody Allen got Mia Farrow, and Burt Reynolds gets all kinds of ladies, and Sylvester Stallone may have muscles but you can't exactly describe him as the world's handsomest man, and his lady is one of the tastiest.

The way you treat your hair is vitally important. Your hair should always be clean and well kempt and very well cut. It's amazing how many men will spend $125 on a pair of shoes, and then begrudge $35 for a haircut. This kind of thinking only makes sense if you walk around with women who are always standing on their heads. Go to the best hairdresser you can find. Travel to the nearest big city if you have to. And make sure that you discuss your hair fully with your stylist before he starts cutting.

The fashion right now is for quite short hair, but the shape of your head and your general life-style will determine how short it's going to be and what kind of a profile you will end up with. Some fundamentals: Broad faces usually take a short style; narrower faces usually need some added "fullness" on the sides. In all cases, however, abandon your preconceptions about what you ought to look like. Fashions change, and although I would never expect you to be a slave to fashion, you should have a fresh, up-to-date look that tells a girl that you're alert and young thinking and that you haven't spent the last few days sawing trees in the backwoods of Oregon.

One of the most important aspects of your hairstyle is that you should feel completely confident with it. That means that you should make sure that your hairstylist cuts it in such a way that it *always* looks good, in wind, rain, or just after you've emerged dripping wet from the swimming pool. Justin, one of Vidal Sassoon's stylists, said, "It's surprising how many men ask for a style which quite obviously doesn't suit their face or their image. They have some-one else in mind—an actor or a rock singer. They think that if they have their hair cut a certain way, it's going to make them look the same."

Of course, it doesn't. You have to make the best of the face you have, and no amount of haircutting can do anything but enhance the looks you were born with. Another point to remember: If your hair is thinning, you should make no attempt to conceal the fact by brushing your hair forward like Julius Caesar or by growing your remaining hair extra long and combing it sideways over the top of your head. Both styles immediately reveal your insecurity about losing your hair, and the last thing you want to do in your first encounter with a woman is reveal any insecurity at all.

You have no need to be insecure. Thinning hair is a natural masculine process, and affirms only that you have a particular type of physiology—not that you're lacking in virility or growing prematurely old. Have your hair cut as short as everyone else, and make sure that you illustrate your age and your style in other ways: in the way you act, in the way you dress, in the way you live your life. I talked to over a hundred women on the subject of men's appearance, and over eighty of them said that thinning hair made no difference whatever to their perception of a man's sexuality. In fact, seven of them said that they thought well-cropped hair on a thinning scalp gave a man "a very attractive, almost frighteningly virile look."

Don't give yourself too elaborate a hairstyle, either (sorry, Elvis fans). These days it's smart to look as if you can afford a good hairstylist, not as if you spend hours in front of store windows combing your hair into a wild style. Think what your hair would look like (a) if you suddenly walked around the corner of a tall building and you were caught by a fierce wind; and (b) if you spent all night making mad passionate love. When you're out with your woman, either eventuality (a) or (b) might hit you when you least expect it, and so have your hair cut sensibly, and take regular care of it.

As far as beards and mustaches go, they're

fine as long as they suit you and are clean and scrupulously trimmed. Some women say they adore the feeling of being given cunnilingus by men with beards and mustaches; others say that they find it "scratchy" and offputting. This is so much a matter of personal taste that you and your lady will have to work it out between you. One small thing, though: Sideburns have gone the way of blue jeans and checkered shirts. They're all right if you're an actual cowboy, but they look hopelessly quaint on the rest of us. These days, whenever you see a man with sideburns, you can guarantee that he still has his whole collection of Everley Brothers singles at home, and that the last car he ever really liked was the 1960 Plymouth Fury. That's what the ladies are going to think, too (at least, those ladies who no longer have beehives).

A small pointer to remember about beards and mustaches: Men who grow them to make themselves look more mature rarely succeed in making themselves look like anything but young men with a false beard on. Men who grow beards in order to hide what they are worried is a "weak chin" rarely succeed in doing anything but highlighting their insecurity about their appearance. The only defensible reason for growing a beard or a mustache is that it makes you look good.

And remember this: you are you. Your appearance is what you are. You have no reason *ever* to lack confidence in the way you look. Everything else we are talking about is concerned simply with fashion and accessories. But they are only the frosting on the cake, nothing more. No amount of hairstyling and Giorgio

Armani jackets can change what you fundamentally are, a modern man who is going out with confidence to find himself the kind of woman he deserves.

What today's woman is looking for is somebody strong but not too strong; somebody well turned out but not vain; somebody considerate but not slavish; somebody sensitive but not mushy; somebody creative but not bizarre; somebody confident but not arrogant; and somebody who, in the words of one very truthful lady, "invites you to dinner, cooks it himself, brilliantly, doesn't try to rope you into helping him by acting incompetent, and refuses your assistance if you ask, leaves the dishes in order to carry you into his bedroom à la Clark Gable, makes love to you passionately and slowly, and afterwards holds you and talks to you into the night."

This same lady admitted that Perfect Tens like this are impossible to find, and would probably be almost unbearable if they could be. But I hope that you get the gist of what women these days are looking for. A man who has character and is self-possessed, yet who takes the trouble to think about her feelings, to put himself in her place.

The way you dress speaks volumes about what you are and what you feel about women. Fashions change so rapidly that it would be fatuous of me to give you any detailed advice on your wardrobe. But check the fashion pages of the more stylish magazines from time to time, just to make sure that the way you look hasn't quietly shuffled into tailoring history. It is always worth owning some classic clothes: an expensive suit, a good blazer, some well-made shirts in pastels and solids. But if you take the trouble to buy something striking and fashionable from time to time, you will stand out as the kind of man who cares about himself—and the kind of man that women would like to be seen with. You don't have to own a vast array of clothes to look good every single day of the week. Just make sure when you go shopping that you buy systematically, that your clothes coordinate with each other in color and fabric. I mean, those maroon pants may look terrific, but how are you going to wear them with that blue plaid coat?

These days, a great many men's clothes are sensibly balanced between formal and casual so that same unstructured coat that you can wear to a poolside party can also look terrific when you wear it to dinner with a wing-collared shirt and a bow tie. There's only one rule with fashion: Do you look good in it? Does it suit your appearance, your coloring, your age? If a man of 40 attempts to wear the same styles as a boy of 18, he will only succeed in betraying his lack of style. You can be 60 and still be fashionable, but you have to take extreme care not to look like mutton dressed up as lamb. Women like older men, but not when those older men are letting their insecurity show. Believe in yourself and what you are. You're chasing women, not rainbows.

Take the trouble to be well groomed. Shave regularly, no matter how those scruffs in television dramas walk around. Keep your nails trimmed and clean. Make sure your teeth are in A-1 condition. Be proud of yourself.

Keep personal jewelry to a minimum. The days when a man proved something about himself by wearing rings on every finger and gold chains around his neck are long gone. A single ring is quite enough; maybe that and an identity bracelet. Use a deodorant, but be sparing with the after-shave. A touch of something dry and severe like Grey Flannel or something light and lemony like Lacoste is quite sufficient to indicate to every woman's nasal passages that you're interested in personal hygiene.

In sum, you can be flamboyant with your clothes, but do try to keep accessories and perfumery to a tasteful minimum.

While we're on the subject of personal hygiene, don't let's forget *intimate* hygiene. Your genital area should also be kept scrupulously clean, particularly if you haven't been circumcised. So too should your anal area. Few women object to the natural sweat aroma that can be exuded after a hard evening's entertaining, dancing, and persuading her to come back to your apartment, any more than you are put off by the natural odor of her genitalia. But regular, twice-daily attention to your ablutions will ensure no wrinkled-up noses on the faces of any of your fair ladies.

One of my greatest beefs for years has been the lack of tissue in public washrooms for men to wipe their penises after urinating. A shake is not enough, not if you want to stay sweet'n'dry. It doesn't do anything for the nation's sexual cleanliness either. The genital area is one area in which you can be proud to be fastidious. Your ladies will always appreciate it.

There was a heated correspondence in *Playboy*

about the trimming of male pubic hair. One woman asked whether she was wrong to demand that her lover shorten the extravagantly long hair that grew on his testicles. Then several men wrote that their wives and girlfriends preferred their pubic hair to be cut shorter, mainly because it looked untidy and because fellatio was so much less choking without it.

Again, this is a matter of personal preference, although I found that over 70 percent of the women I interviewed expressed an interest in seeing their lovers or husbands trimmed or even completely shaved.

Noreen, 24, from White Plains, New York, has taken matters into her own hands. "I always shaved my own pubic hair from the age of 16 or 17 for no other reason except that my mother always did and I preferred it. I think my mother did it because my father liked it, but I didn't see any harm in that and I still don't. I found when I first dated boys that they absolutely flipped when they found out that my vulva was completely bare; it really used to turn them on. And I think I must have had more head from my boyfriends in one semester than any of my friends had in three years. I suppose because of that I was always very much into oral sex. . . . When Gordon and I were first dating, we used to spend whole afternoons going down on each other, and then one day when we were lying in bed I said, 'You know, this really isn't fair, I'm all shaved but you're not. I feel like I'm sucking at a bush.' So in the end I took Gordon to the bathroom, and I made him stand naked in the bath, and I cut his hair real close with nail scissors. Then I soaped his cock and his balls, and I shaved all of his pubic hair off. He had this enormous hard-on while I was doing it, and I kept rubbing his cock slowly up and down just to tease him. When I was finished, I rinsed him off with the shower hose, and there he was, and I loved it, and I still do. The sight of a man's fully developed cock, completely hard, completely shaved bare is really exciting. . . . You suddenly realize how much is usually hidden by hair. I wouldn't let him get out of the bath until I'd sucked his cock and slid my mouth up and down the shaft of it, and I could even pop his balls into my mouth because they weren't hairy anymore. I sucked him until he shot off, all over my breasts, and I knelt up and I smeared his naked cock all over my breasts, with his own sperm to lubricate it. I always shave him now; it makes me feel that he belongs to me in a funny way. It's hard to describe, and our lovemaking feels much better. Until you've felt a completely naked cock going into a completely naked vulva, you haven't felt anything."

Not everybody would agree with Noreen's opinion that "you haven't felt anything," but there is a widespread trend among young women to depilate the so-called "bikini area"—initially because of today's high-cut swimsuits and exercise wear, but afterwards because their lovers have expressed a liking for it. Something about it gives the body the appearance of being more naked than naked, a kind of extra sexual exposure. As Pauline Reage mentions in *The Story of O*, "Only effigies of savage goddesses displayed so high and so visibly the cleft of the sex between whose outer set of lips appeared the crest of the finer inner set . . . O recalled the plump red-haired girl who had told her that her master . . . liked her to be entirely shaven, since only in this way did she appear entirely naked."

Many women have confessed to me that they would enjoy a similar feeling of "entire nakedness" if their husbands or lovers were to be depilated, too. "Sex is equal these days, isn't it?" asked Christa, 31, from Butte, Montana. "Women are still sex objects, and the reason for that is they *like* being sex objects. But now men can be sex objects, too."

You have been warned! But if you're going to be treated as a sex object, you might as well be a terrific-looking sex object. So do take care to be smart, reasonably fashionable, and immaculately groomed. Taking care of your appearance and your personal hygiene will give you confidence and help you to relax; and for most women these are two of the most desirable characteristics in the men they love to love.

What does a woman look for when you first meet her? How can you attract her attention, and keep it? How can you develop a casual meeting into a much more meaningful encounter? Here are some views from women themselves.

Kelly, 22, from New York City, said: "I like a man who shows me that he's interested in me without any kind of hesitation. He should smile, he should ask me something. It shouldn't be anything stupid or weird. Some men seem to think they have to say something incredibly original to catch your attention, but most girls aren't interested in how clever the guy's conversation is, they're only interested in whether the guy's interested in *them*. So a question is always much better than a statement, especially when the question is something about *me*."

Davina, a 26-year-old secretary from St. Louis, agrees: "I cannot bear men who come on too strong, like they're acting in a movie or something. They ought to realize that Richard Gere and all these people they see on the screen are only fantasies, and most women don't want a man who acts that way in any case. It's just laughable to see these men go through the whole routine of leaning against the bar in this casual macho pose, and lighting a cigarette one-handed, and staring at you through slitted eyes. It's an act, and who wants a man who has to act to show you that he likes you? To me, a man who has to act is showing me nothing else except that he's scared to come on like himself. They say things like 'Let's you and me boogie together,' and the next thing you know they've got their hand up your skirt. If they could just see themselves. If they could just hear themselves. They're *painful*."

Sarah, a 24-year-old medical assistant from Los Angeles said, "The men who impress me the most when I first meet them are the men who immediately start to take care of me. Not fussily, I don't mean fussily. But they ask if I've got everything I need, would I like another drink, and in general they show that they're in charge of everything that's going on around them. I'm a very independent lady, I don't let any man tell me what to do, not even the man I love. But a man's presence is essential in every woman's life—well, let's say in *most* women's lives—because we still have a natural biological need to be protected and cared for, even though we're mentally and socially and financially on an equal footing."

On the whole, most women seem to be antagonistic to arrogant, over-the-top come-on lines, although I have seen women respond to some of these lines in practice simply because they've been said with style and panache and wit. If you think you can carry off lines like, "You know what you've done? I have to dismiss my whole harem. None of them can hold a candle to you," then by all means go ahead and give it your best shot. But come-on lines have to sound spontaneous, not as if you've been anxiously practicing them in front of the mirror for three days.

Some men can get away with lines that are highly suggestive, too, such as "I've been standing to attention ever since you came into the room; can I stand at ease for a little while?" But you have to be very careful with lines like these. More often than not they will cause offense, particularly if you've never met the lady before, and you will be exposed as a man whose naked lust happens to be showing just a little too prominently.

May we also *not* say, "Let's fuck, baby?" or "What a great pair of Zeppelins you've got there, sugar?" I'm all for honesty in everyday relationships, but it would be pleasant to think that we had managed to elevate the tone of come-on lines beyond the totally Neanderthal. Apart from that, we will all be less likely to be smacked in the mouth by outraged women who feel that come-on lines like that are degrading both to the person who says them and the person who's being approached.

Time and time again, it is the interested question that works quickest and best. The question can be quite straightforward and innocent. You can reveal a great deal of your interest in the lady with your facial expression and general manner. The important thing is not so much to dazzle her with your amazing audacity and knowledge, but just to get a viable conversation going, a conversation that isn't going to dry up after five minutes into fixed grins and shuffling feet and the woman looking nervously around to see if there's somebody else she can talk to. You see, while you may be equipped with the greatest come-on line known to all mankind, a come-on line only takes a maximum of five seconds to utter, and after that you've got the rest of the evening to fill with lively, absorbing, entertaining, flattering conversation.

On the whole, it's enough for you to keep up-to-date with the more controversial stories in the news, and think out your opinions on them so that you'll always have something topical and reasonably intelligent to say. If it's worth rehearsing anything, rehearse two or three funny personal anecdotes, stories that will amuse her and will also fill in your background as an interesting individual. It's quite legitimate to "doctor" your anecdotes a little, to make them more amusing, but don't borrow too heavily from "Life's Like That" in the *Reader's Digest.* She may be a reader, too.

Rule of good lovership number 304: Never try to tell a woman jokes. Women do not like jokes. The second you start to say, "Y'know, there were these three Mohican Indians . . ." she will go into a glazed state of total boredom. So, please, keep the jokes for the boys' night out.

Rule of good lovership number 305: If a woman makes it clear to you that she isn't interested in your advances, respond with a smile and good grace. One of the most obvious indications of sexual insecurity is the man who persists when a woman says no. Clara, 36, from Wichita, Kansas, said: "One boyfriend I had used to follow me from room to room, saying, '*Why* won't you sleep with me tonight? *Why* won't you sleep with me tonight?' And he would never believe that I just didn't happen to feel like it. In the end, we'd have to spend four exhausting hours analyzing our relationship. The only thing that was wrong with our relationship was his refusal to be confident about it, and to accept that sometimes I was busy and tired and not in the mood for fucking."

Joan, 27, from Boston, said, "I went to a party once and I was having a good time until this guy came up and winked at me and said I had the most terrific thighs he'd ever seen. I just gave him a cold smile and said thank you and ignored him, but he kept on telling me how sexy my hair was, how delicious my lips were, how deep my cleavage was. In the end I screamed at him at the top of my voice, 'Leave me alone, dickhead!' and everybody looked around and of course as far as I was concerned the whole party was ruined. All he did was stand in the middle of the room and grin at everybody and say, 'Can you believe that woman?' So just because he didn't have any class or any style, I was the one who ended up embarrassed. Believe me, if we're talking about come-ons here, that is definitely not the way to win the woman of your choice."

Creative persistence can be rewarded, however. Women do appreciate the man who shows that he's really interested by trying again. Provided you weren't downcast and petulant when she first turned you down, you're certainly permitted a few more valiant tries.

"I met John at the Phoenix airport," said Lucy, a 32-year-old fashion buyer. "He came over and smiled and said, 'I don't have a single rare orchid to give you, like they do in the TV commercials, but could I buy you a drink?' We talked for a while, he was very easygoing and relaxed, he didn't push me or anything. When it was time for my flight, he shook my hand and told me how good it was to have talked to me, and could we meet up next time he was in New York? Well, I was living with Freddie then, and I didn't think that meeting another man was going to be a very good idea, so I said no, it had been pleasant having a drink with him, but I didn't think so. He said okay, maybe I can call you and persuade you to change your mind, and that's how we left it. But six weeks later I found him waiting outside my office after work, and he gave me a single orchid in a celluloid box, and said, 'Here it is. I'm sorry it took so long.' I liked the way he didn't lean on my feelings, I liked the way he kind of knocked and asked admission to my life, and didn't try to tear the door down. He also turned out to be just as good in bed, but that's another story."

When you first date a woman, take care not to be too extravagant. Samantha, 27, a film editor from Los Angeles, told me that when she had first been taken out by an insurance executive named Gerald, seven years her senior, he had taken her to L'Ermitage for dinner, and then presented her with a Baume & Mercier watch that had probably cost $800. "I was very impressed, but I was embarrassed too, and just a tad uncomfortable. I had the feeling that he was buying me rather than courting me. I went to bed with him, yes. He was good-looking and charming, and after all he'd given me a marvelous dinner and spent a whole lot of money on me. But only three weeks later I met a young picture framer called Ned who asked me out for dinner, and when he turned up at my apartment he was carrying a hamper and a folding table, and he set up a whole picnic on my balcony. He'd cooked everything himself, game pie, salad, smoked-salmon mousse, and there was cold pink champagne to go with it. It probably cost him a twentieth of that meal at L'Ermitage, but I loved it, and I loved the thought that he liked me enough to take the trouble to do it. We didn't make love that evening. Well, after Gerald, I'd made myself a promise that I wouldn't have sex on a first date ever again. But Ned didn't mind, and we saw each other twice more before we went to bed together."

So—the tone that women like the best is cool, confident, creative, and caring. Remember, though, that you can't always be perfect, and no woman is going to expect you to be. It's the mistakes you make that show that you're human.

Okay, you've struck up a marvelous and animated conversation with this pretty lady; you like her and she likes you. She accepts your offer of a cocktail, and accepts your offer of a ride home. You reach her house and it's time for a good-night kiss. Now think about it: Do you know how to kiss?

One of the most forceful complaints that women make about men is that they don't. The most common error: They're too slobbery, all wet and overwhelming from the word go. The second most common error: They thrust their tongues immediately into the girl's mouth: "And if that's how they kiss, what are they like when they fuck?" A third error: too much activity, licking and smacking and wiggling their tongues around and not taking the time to relish the moment.

So remember, men. Start your kissing slow and gentle, but be firm and authoritative. Don't peck like a parrot. Don't immediately open your mouth, and when you do, don't stretch it open too wide—you're making love, not visiting the orthodontist. Use your lips to begin with; they are sensitive and feel good. Kiss her lips, kiss her cheeks, kiss her chin, kiss her neck. Build the passion gradually. Tease her a little by kissing her around the earlobes, until her mouth comes searching for yours. Then you can lick and nibble, you can gently draw her lower lip into your mouth, you can run the tip of your tongue across her front teeth.

All the time you're kissing, stay alert to how aroused she's becoming. There's no need for you to hurry, no matter how passionate you feel, and she will be judging your prospects as a lover by this first kiss, just as you will be judging hers. If you're too hasty, too slipshod, too weak, too wet, you may be killing a great sexual relationship before it's even begun. Escalate the eroticism of your kisses only when you feel her respond. Take charge and remain in charge. This is your first physical encounter and somebody has to pace it and she will prefer it if it's you.

Caress her while you're kissing her, but tenderly. Don't let your fingers run ahead of your mouth, or you could scare her away. Hold her and make her feel that you enjoy the closeness of her. So many men allow their accelerating lust to spoil what started off as a well-managed, well-controlled seduction.

Never stuff your tongue down her throat as if you're trying to fuck her in the mouth with it. She may tolerate it at the time, but an overwhelming majority of women listed this maneuver as their number-one offputter. "I thought he was trying to choke me. I almost panicked." "I got the feeling he wanted to lick my liver, he went down so far."

How you carry on after your first kisses will largely depend on where you are, what kind of a mood you're both in, whether there's a bed or a sofa or a comfortable rug handy, and how you're responding to each other. Let's suppose for the sake of argument that she appears to be eager and willing, and that there's a gilded four-poster in the room with the sheets already turned down, and that nobody is going to disturb you for the next few hours. This rarely happens, believe me, but I think you're man enough to find yourself a place to make love, even if you're out in the woods. *Especially* if you're out in the woods.

Caress her body through her clothes. Gently

fondle her breasts, and see if you can locate her nipples through her dress or blouse. Continue to kiss her and to show her how attracted you feel toward her. Then unbutton her buttons, *deftly*, and take off her clothes. If you have trouble with teensy buttons and hook-and-eye catches, you're going to have to practice. Nothing is more offputting than being told by an impatient lady, "Here— let me do it!" while you're butter-fingering her bra catch. Bra catches slide sideways, remember (you *do* remember?). Ease the tension on the strap and slide the upper part of the catch over the inner part so that the hooks-and-eyes disengage. Slip the straps off her shoulders. Discard the bra. Caress her bare breasts. Do not stare at her breasts open-mouthed, no matter how enormous they are, and say, "Gee whillikers, what a pair!" But you are permitted to look, and comment suitably. You are actively encouraged to kiss her nipples, as long as you're not standing up at the time: then you rather tend to look as if you're bending to kiss the Pope's ring.

A skirt may have a similar hook-and-eye catch at the waistband. Again, slide the catch sideways, then tug down the zipper. If she's wearing panties underneath, it sometimes adds to the erotic tension if you fondle her through her panties before taking them off, and slip them to one side.

When you undress yourself, always make sure that you take your socks off first. There is no sillier sight in Christendom than a naked man wearing nothing but his socks, yet time and time again men rip everything off and forget about their argyles. So, it's socks, shirt, pants, shorts. Be quick, but don't tear everything off as if you're rushing to rescue a drowning man in a fast running river.

A brief word about shorts: Keep a fresh wardrobe of regularly replaced shorts. These days, boxers are fashionable for men of all ages, and apart from being fashionable, they flatter the waistline for those of us who don't have rock-hard abdomens. Avoid bizarre underwear—lurex pouches, black leather briefs, orange nylon bikinis—and more than anything else make sure that your underwear is always new and well laundered. Fashions may change, but there is no room in anybody's love life for shriveled elastic.

Well, here you are. You're in bed with her. The mood is passionate, the night is young. All you have to do is remember what I told you about what she expects out of you in bed, and you're off and running.

At the beginning of this book I talked about the Ten Greatest Turn-ons (which we've already discussed in Chapter 5), but I also mentioned the Ten Greatest Turn-offs. We'd better swallow hard and get these over with, chaps, and if we're guilty even of one of them, we'd better place our right hand over our heart and swear never *ever* to be guilty of them again.

These turn-offs have not been extrapolated from a nationwide survey, but the women who listed them formed a cross section of the nation and different walks of life, and so their remarks lead to interesting, if nonscientific, conclusions. Lack of *personal hygiene* comes unassailably first. That means dirty untrimmed fingernails, dirty dandruffy hair, unpleasant body odor, shaving cream still clinging in the ears. Lack of *clothes maintenance* comes second, the famous soup-stained tie, the filthy Nike trainers, the unpressed pants, the shirt that looks as if you've been wearing it nonstop for five days, the once-smart suede coat that is now greasy and bald. *Bad teeth* are considered to be highly offputting. It's worth having those discolored front teeth capped; at least you'll look kissable again. *Overpossessiveness* comes close to bad teeth, for some reason: women don't like their men to hover around them too much when they go to parties or social gatherings, and they don't like being bullied or nagged into keeping away from other men. Their feeling (quite rightly) is that this displays a lack of confidence in their fidelity, and also a lack of confidence in your ability to keep them happy. The old *overpowering aftershave* is another no-no. Are we going to give that bottle of Brut to the thrift store, gentlemen? Yes, we are. A *filthy automobile* is another serious criticism. If a woman dresses smartly to go on a date, she doesn't enjoy being driven around in a dusty vehicle with crammed-full ashtrays and a backseat littered with old Chinese take-out boxes. General *courtesy and etiquette* comes in for a whole lot of flak. Men who open doors, always walk on the outside of the sidewalk, always draw restaurant chairs out, help their ladies into their coats, ask if they might smoke, eat with the right knives and forks, and do their best to give their women an orgasm—these men, I'm sorry to say, are not as thick on the ground as they ought to be. We will smarten up, won't we?

Sexual turn-offs came quite low on the totem

pole of complaints. But without a doubt the worst of these sins was *roughness*—handling a woman as if she were a steer to be branded rather than a soft and sensitive human being. "Geoff used to push his fingers up me when I was still dry. It was so uncomfortable and unromantic." "Walt was the world's worst breast-grabber. I don't know what he thought they were made of, but he used to seize hold of them and twist them around until sometimes I had to fight him off." "He used to come thundering down on top of me, fuck me immediately, roaring away like a bull elephant, come, and then collapse so heavily that I couldn't breathe."

Lack of *anatomical knowledge* was another problem, particularly in the genital area. Many men had only the vaguest idea what the clitoris looked like and exactly where it was located, and most thought they could handle it as if it were a smaller version of their own penis. A remarkable number of men were not aware that a woman's urethra was separate from her vagina. As Gay Talese remarked in his book *Thy Neighbor's Wife*: "Talese . . . saw several S&M films [with] high-heeled goddesses flailing men with whips, squeezing their genitals, and not infrequently squatting over the body of a prone man and urinating in his face. Whatever else might be said of such scenes, Talese guessed that many men found the scenes of squatting women sexually educational, for Talese had long theorized that most men of his generation had no idea that a woman urinated from a different opening than the one she used for making love."

Last of all (and rather contradictory in a way, considering how important an emphasis women placed on personal hygiene) the tenth greatest turn-off is the man who insists before making love on folding all his clothes properly, placing his shoes side by side under the end of the bed, winding his watch, cleaning his teeth, brushing his hair, applying underarm deodorant, removing his contact lenses and putting them in to soak, and switching off the light. Perhaps husbands can be forgiven for such ritual behavior after several years of marriage, but as 37-year-old Petra said, "Sometimes I just want him to take me to bed and fuck me, and to hell with putting the cat out."

8.
Trouble in Paradise—AIDS and Other Problems

When I wrote *How to Be the Perfect Lover* ten years ago, the Sexual Revolution was in full swing, sexual-encounter groups and singles bars were thriving, and there was literally nothing to discourage anybody from having sex with anybody else except the familiar treatable venereal diseases and (of course) personal preference.

The emergence of AIDS has changed all that. These days, casual sexual relationships are approached with far more caution, and those bisexuals who were once welcomed into group-sex scenes with both men and women are now finding themselves ostracized. There is no need for me to underline the agony that has been suffered by the gay community.

You should think seriously about AIDS if you are a single man who is going out to form casual sexual relationships with women, and particularly if you are considering having sex with prostitutes. You should think equally seriously about AIDS if you are a married man who might conceivably find himself having sexual relations with a woman not his wife—whether it is likely to happen accidentally or deliberately.

You can take certain simple and sensible precautions to protect yourself from AIDS, however, even though research into the AIDS virus is still in its infancy, and there are still many questions about how it is transmitted.

What is known is that AIDS is a blood disease, and that only blood and semen can carry it from one person to another. There have been isolated cases wherein the baby of a nursing mother has been given AIDS through breast milk, and there are theories that it can be carried by mosquitoes from one human to another. But the main point to remember is that the virus has to be given access to your bloodstream before it can infect you. You can't catch AIDS from kissing an AIDS sufferer; you can't catch AIDS from drinking glasses or toilet seats or taxi door-handles.

The reason that so many homosexuals have contracted the AIDS virus is that during anal intercourse the delicate tissues inside the rectum are frequently torn, and so infected semen comes directly into contact with the bloodstream. The principal cause of AIDS being transmitted among heterosexuals is through the use of infected hypodermic needles during what is delicately called "recreational drug use," or through blood transfusions with infected blood.

The truth of the statement that AIDS is a blood disease and not a sexual disease can be seen by contrasting the statistics in the United States and Africa. In the United States, well over 10,500 homosexual men have contracted AIDS, compared with only 150 heterosexual men—and out of those 150 heterosexual men, only 19 of them were given AIDS by a woman.

Anal intercourse—one infected man sodomizing another—is one of the few ideal breeding grounds for AIDS. Mathilde Krim, who heads up the AIDS Medical Foundation, said recently, "The virus is very difficult to transmit. In order to infect, it must be freshly out of a live, transmitting cell, and it must almost immediately meet a specific white blood cell on its surface. In other words there must be an open cut with hot fresh blood. It cannot be spread through ordinary physical contact."

In Africa general standards of hygiene are extremely low, and in Central Africa where AIDS has reached almost epidemic proportions, most medical treatment is carried out by administering injections, often with infected needles. The incidence of AIDS is therefore almost as high among women as among men. AIDS is further spread throughout the continent by indiscriminate sex between homosexuals and heterosexuals, and widespread prostitution.

The simple precautions that you can take against contracting AIDS are these:

> Avoid having sex with prostitutes. Apart from the contact they may have had with AIDS sufferers, prostitution is clearly associated with drugs, and the chances of the prostitute herself carrying the AIDS virus are high.
>
> Avoid having sex with women whom you know or suspect may also be having sex with homosexuals or with drug addicts.

When you have sex with a woman whose sexual history you are not 100 percent confident of, use a condom. Make sure that your brand of condoms is reliable.

Avoid using sexual aids that may have been used by somebody else (such as dildoes and anal vibrators). If you insist on using them, make sure that you wash them thoroughly first.

Educate the women with whom you have sex in the ways they can avoid contracting and spreading AIDS. Advise them to make sure that any other sex partners they may have are not also having sex with men, or with drug-addicted women or prostitutes. Advise them also to give up anal intercourse.

It is reasonably safe for a woman to enjoy anal intercourse if her partner wears a condom and uses plenty of KY jelly to avoid tearing her rectal tissues, but less safe than not doing it at all.

If you know any gay men, or if you have any gay connections yourself, there are some pretty rigid rules that *must* be observed. The first is to stop having mouth-to-anus sex, and to give up anal intercourse. Fellatio is okay provided men don't ejaculate into each other's mouths. Masturbation is all right; so is kissing; but what the anti-AIDS campaigners discreetly call "the exchange of bodily fluids" is absolutely out.

For some gay men giving up anal intercourse would be almost impossible. It would be as drastic as asking a straight man to give up vaginal intercourse. If a man really can't live without it, then he must *always* use a condom, and make every effort he can to ensure that his sex partners do not come from a high-risk group, like drug addicts or very promiscuous gays.

AIDS is a drastic and terrible disease. When the AIDS virus enters your bloodstream, it invades your white cells and makes them produce more of the AIDS virus. When all of your white cells have been attacked, your body's immunity system ceases to function, and you become prey to any illnesses that may be floating around, many of which can prove fatal. The AIDS virus can also attack your central nervous system, with disastrous consequences.

There are two mistaken reactions to AIDS. The first is to panic, and to avoid hysterically all contact with anyone who might remotely be carrying the virus in their bloodstream. This does nothing but make it more difficult for you and everyone around you to come to terms with the reality of it and to propagate calmly and quietly the real facts about the virus (as far as they're known). Anytime anyone mentions AIDS, you should make a point of emphasizing that it is a contamination of the blood, not a sexual disease, and you should repeat the precautions that I have listed above. One more person educated is one less person at risk.

The second wrong reaction is to use the what-the-hell argument of the type used by cigarette smokers and those who regard buckling up as an infringement of their constitutional rights. These are the folks who are going to continue fucking anybody they please in any way they please, without any consideration for those who might suffer as a result, including themselves.

Unfortunately, many men in the high-risk group take this attitude—promiscuous homosexuals and drug addicts—and they are just the people who are helping to spread AIDS the most.

Research into AIDS is progressing quickly, and some kind of immunization against it may be found within a year or two. Meanwhile, however, you can make your contribution to stamping it out (and also to protecting your own health) by following the guidelines. I agree that they do take a certain *frisson* out of sexual encounters, but if you have any doubts at all that you're doing the right thing, think back on those newspaper photographs of Rock Hudson in the last stages of his illness, and say to yourself, "That's not going to happen to me, period."

While we're on the grim subject of AIDS, it's worth mentioning that all sexually transmitted diseases have been on the increase worldwide. The most common are gonorrhea, syphilis, non-specific urethritis, genital warts, herpes, and trichomoniasis vaginalis. It's worth giving a brief description of them—not for the purpose of turning you off sex but simply so that you'll recognize them if you do happen to have the misfortune to come into contact with them.

The absolute rule with all disorders of the sexual organs is: Speed to your doctor at the very first opportunity and have yourself treated. Your doctor won't make any moral judgments. All he's interested in is treating you (and also making sure that whoever you've been having sex with is also treated) and keeping sexually transmitted diseases down to a minimum. Concern in the medical profession about sexually transmitted diseases has been so strong that in 1961 the U.S. Public Health Department set up a special task force to track down and eradicate every case of syphilis they could.

These are the most widespread venereal diseases and their symptoms:

1. **Gonorrhea:** transmitted by a bean-shaped bacterium called a *gonococcus* during sexual intercourse or genital contact. It cannot be carried on toilet seats because it rapidly dies if deprived of the warmth and moisture of the human body. Men with gonorrhea notice a discharge of pus from the penis, sufficient to soil their underwear, and they may experience a burning pain when urinating. After a week the whole length of the urethra becomes inflamed. If unattended, gonorrhea may lead to abscesses in the urethra, infection of the prostate gland, and gonococcal epididymitis, in which men suffer a hard red swelling about the size of a tennis ball, and which frequently leads to scars in the epididymis so serious that sperms are no longer able to reach the urethra from the testicle, rendering a man sterile. Unfortunately, the presence of gonorrhea in women is far more difficult to detect, which is why women often spread it from partner to partner before they have any inkling what might be wrong. The symptoms of gonorrhea in women (a slight burning sensation when urinating, heavy vaginal discharge) can easily be mistaken for the symptoms of noncommuni-

cable problems like cystitis. Gonorrhea is treated with penicillin or other antibiotics.

2. **Syphilis** is a much more serious disease than gonorrhea and much more internationally widespread. It can cause extreme illness and even death. It is caused by a corkscrew-shaped germ called *Treponema pallidum*, which, like the gonococcus, requires warmth and moisture in order to survive and dies quickly when exposed even to the mildest of antiseptics. This is why it is almost always transmitted sexually. The first sign of syphilis is a primary sore that appears at the point of sexual contact, usually on or around the genitals. In homosexuals it can first appear on the anus or even inside the rectum. In women it tends to appear first of all on the cervix, the neck of the womb, well out of sight, and so women can be highly infectious without realizing it. The primary sore is usually hard and rubbery and not particularly painful. In the second stage of the disease the glands in the groin become enlarged, and within a week the treponemes enter the bloodstream and insinuate their way into every organ in the body. The telltale symptoms of this stage of the disease are a coppery skin rash, as well as sores in the mouth. After three or four years, however, the body's immune system manages to eliminate the rash for good, and the syphilis sufferer becomes noninfectious. However, unless the syphilis has been diagnosed and treated, it now en-

ters its third dormant stage, in which it may remain for anywhere between five and fifty years. Eventually, it will reappear in its fourth stage, in severe forms that can cripple or even kill. It can bring on heart disease, paralysis, blindness, and syphilitic insanity. Provided it is identified in time, syphilis is cured by penicillin and other antibiotics. Even men and women suffering from the fourth stage can have their condition arrested by penicillin.

3. **Nonspecific urethritis** (NSU) produces similar symptoms to gonorrhea but is not spread by the gonococcus, and in 90 percent of cases the cause is unknown. It is transmitted during sexual intercourse, like gonorrhea, but takes longer to incubate. Men will notice an inflammation of the urethra, as well as a discharge through the penis, and a frequent urge to urinate. A broad spectrum of antibiotics is effective against NSU, but if ignored it can produce skin rashes, arthritis, sores, and inflamed eyes. In women NSU is far more difficult to detect, and a woman can infect her sexual partner without even realizing that she is carrying the condition. Whenever a man discovers that he has NSU, he should immediately tell any women with whom he has been having sex, since the disease can eventually cause damage to a woman's fallopian tubes and sterilize her.

4. **Genital warts** are often linked with other venereal diseases, since they flourish in

the moist discharge associated with gonorrhea and syphilis and vaginitis. They are caused by a skin virus, and they can grow both internally and externally. In men they grow under the foreskin and along the shaft of the penis, and also around the anus. They are extremely infectious, and up to 10 percent of people treated for venereal diseases are found to have genital warts as well. The warts are treated by swabbing with chemicals and by powdering them to keep them dry. In chronic cases, however, they may have to be removed surgically.

5. **Herpes genitalis** is caused by another virus, part of the same family that produces cold sores. The early symptoms of herpes are irritating red patches on the skin, which soon break out into small itchy blisters. Eventually these form tiny ulcers that can resemble the early stages of syphilis. There is no effective cure for herpes, and fear of contracting it has led to many men curtailing their extramarital sexual activities. It has also encouraged herpes sufferers, both men and women, to advertise for infected partners. Herpes genitalis may disappear for a while, but it almost always recurs.

6. **Trichomoniasis** is a tiny one-celled parasite that infests the vagina, causing a severe vaginal discharge. Occasionally it invades the urethra and the glands around it, producing symptoms that can easily be mistaken for cystitis. If a man has repeatedly had sexual intercourse with a

woman suffering from trichomoniasis, he can develop a discharge from the penis not unlike urethritis, but while they can carry the parasite from one woman to another, men do not usually display any symptoms. Trichomoniasis can quickly be cured by a single course of metronidazole tablets.

Unpleasant as the discussion of venereal diseases can be, there is no escaping the fact that they proliferated and spread during the years of the Sexual Revolution, and that any man who is considering sexual relations with women with whom he is not familiar should understand that he is exposing himself to a percentage risk of infection. Not all guys are as sexually fastidious as you, and no matter how beautiful and well mannered that lady may appear to be, she may be carrying something invisible that you don't want to catch. She may not even be aware that she is carrying it.

At its least malevolent, venereal disease is uncomfortable. At its most malevolent, it can break up relationships, finish marriages, and bring on painful and long-lasting illness and even death.

You have a personal responsibility to yourself and to all of your sexual partners to make sure that sexually transmitted diseases don't spread. Knowing what symptoms to look for, and knowing what damage VD can do, is all part of being a good lover.

Happiness is not only a good dinner, a bout of love that makes your ears ring, and a Krakatoa of a climax. Happiness is healthiness too.

9

A Taste of Honey—How to Be Expert at Oral Sex

Cunnilingus—the arousal of a woman with your mouth and tongue—is one of the most useful and practical sexual variations known to man, and is certainly one of the most stimulating experiences known to woman.

The terrific thing about cunnilingus is that you can use it to bring your woman to a climax quite independently of your erection (or lack of erection). You can use it as a way of arousing your woman before intercourse, as a way of making sure that your woman is satisfied after intercourse, or as a substitute for intercourse.

Although many women are still shy of cunnilingus (and even shocked by it), it has an ancient and venerable history as a sexual technique, and its sexual and social importance can be judged from sculptures and paintings from all over the world, dating back to primitive times, in which men and women are depicted in the throes of "69." On the temples at Rajarani and

Konarak in India, voluptuous figures are enthusiastically licking at each other's wide-open *yonis;* and erotic playing cards made in Dahomey in the nineteenth century depict every conceivable position for oral sex.

Enthusiastic descriptions of cunnilingus appear in literature too, from ancient to modern. Here's a short excerpt from a nineteenth-century "gentleman's magazine": "Excited by the wine, and madly lustful to enjoy the dear girls to the utmost, I stretched Sophie's legs wide apart, and sinking on my knees, gamahuched her virgin cunt, till she spent again in ecstasy, whilst dear Annie was doing the same to me, sucking the last drop of spend from my gushing prick. Meanwhile, Frank was following my example. Rosa surrendered to his lascivious tongue the recesses of her virginity as she screamed with delight and pressed his head toward her mount when the frenzy of love brought her to the spending-point."

Compared with the bawdiness of that excerpt, this fictitious account of cunnilingus from a modern magazine called *Playbirds Continental* seems almost tame, but the erotic effect of the technique is still the same (notice, incidentally, the sheer quantity of female fluids; our writers of erotica still haven't learned!): "Two naked women. Janet was one of them, her cunt lips already pouting with pleasure, already dripping with juice, and the other girl was just as beautiful, and she had shaved all her cunt hair off and her lips were just as pouting, just as wet. Lana reached down, yes, both her hands went to her cunt, and then she spread them wide, spread them very wide. It was lovely to watch

Lana finger herself, lovely to see the love juices go dripping down all over Janet's face, and of course Janet had her mouth wide open and she was drinking those juices down as fast as she could go!"

I am all in favor of erotic fiction, but I do desperately wish sometimes that it would be sexually accurate. Any man who had not tried cunnilingus would expect from those excerpts to be flooded with juice as soon as he went down on his woman; and any woman who had not been licked by a man would expect to drown the poor fellow before the evening was out.

Those women who are cautious about oral sex are usually those who have never had a man look closely at their vulvas, or who feel that there is something dirty and disgusting about men stimulating their genitals with their mouths.

Jenny Fabian, a well-known "groupie" of the 1960s, and an arch-proponent of giving men head, once told me that in spite of the fact that she had fellated innumerable rock stars, she couldn't stand the idea of a man staring at her between her legs.

This is Geraldine, 24, from San Francisco: "The first man who ever 'went down' on me was a guy called Jimmy I met at a cookout in Sausalito. I was just 20 at the time, and I wasn't very sexually experienced. In fact, I wasn't very experienced at anything. I think I'd had three boyfriends and slept with two of them, once in a darkened bedroom and once on the beach under a blanket. Jimmy was a painter, and he had a studio on top of an old bookstore. There were huge paintings everywhere, mostly naked women, and about four mattresses laid out on the floor to make a vast bed that you could really roll around on. We met at the cookout and drank some good wine and got talking; and then we danced; and then he asked me back to his place. He was tall and very thin and he had a beard. He looked kind of like John the Baptist, very biblical. We drank some more wine, and then he took off my clothes very slow, and laid me down on all these mattresses. I remember I was quite excited because all the lights were still on, and I could see him naked, with his bright red cock sticking up out of his bushy black hair. There were hurricane lamps all around the mattresses; it was as bright as daylight. He kissed me, my mouth and my neck, and he played with my breasts, and we were both pretty worked up by then, so he took his cock in his fist and he pushed it up between my legs. I said, 'I never made love with the lights on before,' and he said, 'Haven't you seen what it looks like?' and he helped me to sit up so that I could watch his great big thick cock sliding in and out of me. I was amazed that I could take so much inside of me; it almost seemed impossible. Although he made love to me beautifully, our rhythms didn't quite synchronize, but that happens, I guess, with someone you don't know too well. He lasted a long time, but he climaxed long before I was ready, even though I was really turned on. The incredible thing was, though, that he didn't hesitate. He didn't hesitate for an instant. He took his cock out of me, and he knelt between my legs and lifted up the cheeks of my bottom with both hands, and he licked me, one huge lick, right from my vagina up to my clitoris. I can remember saying 'No, don't,' and trying to twist away, but he held me tight and he wouldn't let me go. He buried his face deep between my legs, I could feel his beard against my thighs, and he licked at my clitoris really fast and light. I was gripping his hair because I was trying to stop him. I kept thinking to myself in total panic, 'This man's actually licking my cunt!' He went on and on, though, and after a while my panic started to die down, and I began to feel these incredible waves of feeling going through me. Suddenly I really didn't want him to stop at all; suddenly I didn't care. His tongue was flying! Then he slid a finger up inside my vagina and began to massage me right inside, and before I knew what was happening I could feel myself coming to a climax. I tried to resist it, but then I couldn't resist it, and it gripped hold of me and I was shaking and jumping around and yelping out loud. He looked up and his lips were shining because he'd been sucking at my vagina, and his eyes were glowing and he looked marvelous. I held him and kissed him, and for the first time in my life I tasted myself, my own juices. It excited me—no, it didn't turn me off. If he could enjoy the taste of it, why couldn't I, and after all it was all intermingled with his."

Once they have experienced cunnilingus, most women enjoy it thoroughly, and find it a highly stimulating part of loveplay. A woman who expresses any reluctance to let you go down on her, however, should be handled with care: The last thing you want to do is put her off the idea of oral sex for good. Introduce it into your love-making gradually, as part of your foreplay, kissing her lips and her shoulders and her breasts and then progressively working your way down. Take your time; don't make a beeline for her vulva after only a couple of peremptory kisses on the lips: A woman likes to think that she's more than just a vagina with a personality attached.

When you first introduce a woman to cunnilingus, go softly. Kiss the outer lips of her vulva without inserting your tongue; then lick at her clitoris very gently with your tongue tip. Don't forget while you're licking that you have hands, and that from your position nestling between her legs you can reach up and caress her breasts and her nipples—that's unless you have exceedingly short arms.

After you have stimulated the clitoris a little, part her outer lips with your tongue (not with your fingers) and probe inside her vulva so that you can open her inner lips. They may be open already, depending on what position she's lying in and how aroused she is, but now you can insert your stiffened tongue into her vagina, and relish the taste of those celebrated juices (although don't expect the sluice gates of the Hoover Dam to open, because even in the juiciest of women they won't).

At this point, after a little in-and-outing with your tongue, you can carefully hold the outer lips of her vulva apart, which will have the effect of exposing her vagina and her clitoris much more prominently. Run your tongue tip back up to her clitoris and lick it softly and steadily and keep on licking it softly and steadily until you can sense that she is beginning to feel aroused. Whatever fancy tricks you do with your tongue and your fingers, it is the persistent rhythmic lapping of your tongue tip on her clitoris that will eventually bring her to a climax, so make sure that you don't ignore it for too long.

Once she is well aroused, you can of course make some downward trips to her vagina again, to taste the flow of her lubricant, and to stimulate intercourse with your tongue. There is, of course, the question of whether you like the taste of your woman's vagina. Most men find the flavor mildly sweet and most arousing. Several aficionados I spoke to pronounced it "the single most delicious taste in the known universe." There is no doubt that sexual inhibitions always melt away when you are highly stimulated, and a flavor that might be bland or disagreeable under normal circumstances can be extremely arousing when you are turned on.

One of the most enthusiastic gourmets of women's vaginas that I have ever come across is Xaviera Hollander, the Happy Hooker, who used to write for me when I worked for *Penthouse* magazine. She once described a Sapphic experience with another woman called Nancy that culminated in a classic bout of cunnilingus.

"I lay in Nancy's arms, feeling the warmth of her body and the rigidity of her distended nipples. I was getting so horny that in another few minutes I thought I would come through sheer mental stimulation. After a few minutes of relaxing and sighing together, I felt her arm rubbing my back. I started to lick her, first her earlobes, then her neck down to her stiffened nipples, then all around her belly button, finally plunging into her delicious pussy as she gasped in pleasure."

Gentlemen, take note. This is a woman describing how to perform cunnilingus with a woman.

"All of this seemed to take an eternity. Her bush was heart-shaped, with the hairs cut fairly short. Holding each leg down with one arm, I started to flick at her clitoris with my tongue. (They don't call me the fastest tongue in town for nothing.) She was soon ready to explode. I bent forward and wrapped my arms around her voluptuous hips and ass. Her thighs seemed divine as I spread them apart and once again I began to eat around the small triangle until I hit the rose. I inserted my index finger deep into her moist cunt, then replaced the finger with my eager tongue.

"This time I moved my tongue very gently. She was so wet that I could really taste the juices from her cunt. I was so lost that I didn't realize that Nancy was trying to lick my clitoris and playing with me with her fingers. She manipulated and vibrated my clitoris in every possible way, then ended up squeezing it until it was almost painful."

During the act of cunnilingus you can exercise extraordinary control over your woman's sexual responses, and can build her up toward a memorable orgasm far more adeptly than you can by using your penis alone. Apart from flicking the clitoris with your tongue, you can gently tug her vaginal lips into your mouth, you can explore her urethra (which lies just below her clitoris), and you can fasten your whole open mouth over her clitoral area, drawing it upward into your mouth with subtle (not fierce or painful) suction, flicking your tongue over her imprisoned clitoris until she climaxes or you run out of breath.

When your woman becomes more relaxed about cunnilingus, you can indulge your taste for her well-stimulated vulva even more extravagantly. This is Karen, 27, a radio station assistant from Phoenix, talking about her love of oral sex: "My live-in boyfriend Philip was the first man ever to give me an orgasm through licking me. I was stunned when it happened. I couldn't believe it. Boys had gone down on me before, but most of the time they hadn't done anything more than fumble around with their tongues and fingers for a while and then come up again. But Philip woke me up one morning by kissing my vagina. I'll never forget it. The sun was coming through the window, all across the bed, and suddenly I felt these lips kissing me between my legs. Then I felt a tongue sliding right into me. I opened my eyes but I didn't move. I just lay there and let him do it, and believe me he was beautiful. He licked my clitoris around and around until it felt like it was standing up like a pencil eraser. Then he pushed his tongue as far as it would go into my vagina. He stretched me apart with his fingers so that he could go deeper. I was pretty wet by then, and I was afraid that he wouldn't like it, but he pushed his face right into my vulva, and smeared his cheeks and his nose and his eyes and his mouth with all of my juices. He truly reveled in it, and then he licked my clitoris again until I could hardly stand the sensation of it any longer. He ran one finger up into my vagina, then another, then another, and then he rubbed my juices all around my anus, and worked his thumb right up into my bottom. He began to masturbate me with his hand, his whole hand, and at the same time he was licking me like wildfire. I remember that orgasm even today. It came at me like a locomotive. I could feel it coming in the distance; then it hit me and it hit me so hard that I think I was actually unconscious for a moment or two. I opened my eyes and there was Philip looking down at me and smiling and his whole face was shining because of the wetness out of my vagina. I said, 'You're mad,' and he said, 'You're delicious.' "

There are men who want to stimulate their women orally, but who really can't accept the taste of vaginal juices. One solution for them is to lick their partners' clitorises but to go no further down. After a while they may find that they grow accustomed to her taste. If not, their own saliva is usually an adequate lubricant.

While women enjoy the attentions of cunnilingus as a part of loveplay, they are less interested in oral sex than men. It is a mistake to assume that just because you have spent time and care and effort bringing your woman to a climax through giving her head, she is automatically going to do the same for you. *Don't* thrust your penis into her face in a silent demand to be cocksucked. Your continued attention to her vulva will encourage her to reciprocate when she is ready. Fellatio (cocksucking) is a very different act from cunnilingus. Not only does it require more manual stimulation to accompany it, but if it goes the whole way through to a climax, it becomes a substitute for intercourse rather than an adjunct—simply because it will take you anything from ten to twenty minutes to be able to rise again and achieve full penetration of her vagina. After cunnilingus, however, a woman can have intercourse immediately. In fact, it can intensify her orgasm if you slide your penis into her while she is still going through the climactic spasms that you have induced through the use of your tongue.

A brief word on fellatio: Many women will either not attempt it at all or will be very half-hearted about it simply because they are not confident that they are doing it right. In other words, they have heard that women put men's penises into their mouths, but they haven't got a clue as to what happens next. If your woman begins to show an inclination to suck your cock, it is incumbent upon you to be demonstrative and educational, not forceful. You should say, "That's gorgeous . . . that's gorgeous, when you do it like that," or gently lift her head if she's sucking too hard. Tell her what to do. It's your penis, she can't feel what you're feeling. It's no good complaining that women are always silent about what turns them on the most if you're just as incommunicative. She wants to be satisfied; she also wants to satisfy you. Make sure that you tell her how.

Of course, one of the biggest questions about fellatio is: Should she swallow your sperm? Should you hold her head while you're coming, and compel her to swallow your sperm? Does it make any difference if she swallows it or not?

Semen contains only simple sugars and protein, and even the most copious ejaculation produces no more than a teaspoonful. It's the spreadability of semen that sometimes makes it seem far more than it actually is. Some women dislike the eggy consistency and bleachy, astringent taste, but many more find it arousing and delicious. Xaviera Hollander recalled fellating a man who had never made love before: "Now I was experiencing his jism shooting out of his cock into my mouth. It was beautiful and warm and plentiful. I half-swallowed it and half-dribbled it onto his belly. I hadn't seen sperm like that, so thick, in a long time. It almost reminded me of yogurt."

In a close sexual relationship most women are happy to taste a little of their partner's semen, but don't be upset if your woman feels disinclined to swallow the whole ejaculation. Madeline, 25, from Austin, Texas, told me: "Henry always expected me to suck down everything whenever I gave him a BJ [blowjob]. He thought that was what a man's woman ought to do, regardless of whether she liked it or not. He used to yell out, 'Suck it clean, suck it clean!' every time I sucked him off, but the truth was that I didn't care for it too much. It used to make me gag, even though I loved Henry just as much as any woman could. So what I got to doing in the end was taking his penis out of my mouth just when he started to come, and let him shoot over my face, all over my hair and my cheeks and my eyelashes, and maybe just a little on my lips, because I did like to lick a little bit. But he liked that much better, he used to love to shoot all over my face, and I know some women think it's degrading, but I'd defend what we do, I think it shows our love for each other strong and true. I love to feel his come on my cheeks, just the same way he goes down on me, and smothers his face. It's just what they say in the marriage ceremony, with my body I thee worship."

The celebrated act of "69"—that is, you licking her while she's sucking you—is to my mind one of the least satisfactory of sexual positions. There are times during your bedtime frolics when it will happen naturally. Your woman will be sucking your cock and you will suddenly find yourself confronted by her wide-open vagina. You will hardly be likely to light a cigarette and pick up a book until she's finished. But cunnilingus and fellatio are special; they are the devotion of one partner to the other's pleasure. As such, they require the concentrated attention of both of you, which cannot be achieved during "69." One of you to concentrate on licking and the other one to concentrate on receiving pleasure. To have to suck or lick somebody else while somebody else is sucking or licking you is like having to circle your head and rub your stomach at the same time. Your brain cannot accept all the input, and in the end you will usually end up exhausted, confused, and dissatisfied. If you want to give your woman cunnilingus, lie between her legs where her mouth cannot reach your penis. She can always fellate you after you've finished, if she wants to. And the act of licking her into an orgasm will give you plenty of indirect stimulation, especially when she climaxes while your tongue is still inside her vagina. Now, that is a sensation in a million—but freely available for all good lovers.

Don't feel reticent about using your fingers to

increase your woman's pleasure during cunnilingus. While you're furiously licking her clitoris, the insertion of one finger or more into her vagina can greatly increase her delight. If you feel like it, you can insert your index finger into her anus (well lubricated by her vaginal juices) while your middle finger probes her vagina. As you lick her steadily toward an orgasm, you can gently "fuck" her vagina and her anus with your fingers, deeply increasing her pleasure.

How readily your woman will accept these stimulations will depend (a) on her own experience, and (b) on how you do them. If your woman has had plenty of experience with other men, she won't be shy about cunnilingus . . . and this will be your opportunity to show her just how good you are. You're not nervous, are you? All you have to do is keep her clitoris lightly flicked and highly stimulated, and you won't have anything to worry about. All the rest of the action is pleasant but superfluous. Do whatever you want, but make sure you keep her building steadily toward that climax.

If she has never experienced cunnilingus before, or only rarely, then you have to be slow, careful, and complimentary. Make her feel that it's something new for you too—which it will be, since every woman's vulva is different, and every woman tastes different. Bring a little of your own wonder to a wonderful act of love.

Cunnilingus isn't a technique to be used every time you make love. Your mood will determine when you want to suck your lady out. But it is an extremely versatile way of driving your woman wild in bed. Try it as part of your foreplay, like Allen, 29, an accountant from Detroit: "I was having some real problems with Shirley. I was beginning to think that we were completely incompatible as far as sex was concerned. She could never reach an orgasm, even if I managed to hold back my climax for ten or fifteen minutes. She always used to say that she was never aroused enough, but I thought, you know, what the hell more can I do? I kiss her, I play with her breasts, I hold her, I bite her tongue, I fondle her clitoris . . . what else is there? But one day, we were sitting on the couch watching television, and Shirley was sitting with her feet up so that her dress had slid down to her waist and her legs were bare. I started stroking her thighs quite absentmindedly, then my hand went down between her legs, and I caressed her pussy through these small red nylon panties she was wearing. She didn't say anything, just smiled, so I kept on stroking her until I could feel through the nylon that she was getting wet and turned on. I knelt down beside the couch and pulled her panties to one side, and kept on fingering her. But then something inspired me to lean forward and kiss her pussy, and lick it a little. I just loved the way it was bulging out from the side of her panties, shining pink flesh, like something good to eat. She held on to my shoulder and said, 'Don't,' but I kept on licking her all around her pussy, and after a while she closed her eyes and I could feel the muscles in her body begin to tighten and I suddenly understood that she was working herself toward an orgasm. Well, that turned me on, too, of course; my prong was almost bursting out of my pants. But I gave all my attention to Shirley. I licked her and licked her until she was murmuring and moaning and her hips were twisting around and then at last she bent forward and started to shake and I knew that she was coming. Right away, I unbuckled my belt and took down my pants and pushed my prong straight up her. She was warm and slippery and she was fantastic. It took only six or seven strokes, and I was ready to climax. I said to Shirley, 'I'm coming,' but she said not yet, not yet, and she took hold of my cock and pulled it out of her pussy and immediately clamped her mouth around it. She only had to move her head up and down two or three times before I climaxed straight into her mouth. She licked around the head of my prong to get the very last drop of it, and I could see the sperm swirling around her tongue and her teeth. I guess that was the beginning of our better times. We both lost some inhibitions that day, and I found out that I could bring her up to a climax before we actually started making love, so she was always guaranteed satisfaction. That reassured me, and my confidence reassured her, so all around we did pretty good."

The eroticism of cunnilingus can be heightened by doing it when it is least expected. Bill, a 27-year-old engineer from Seattle, likes to wake his wife up in the morning by licking her vulva: "And she likes it, too. She says it's a much better way of waking up than any old alarm clock." Richard, 31, a computer programmer from Charleston, South Carolina, once gave his wife cunnilingus while she was talking to her sister on the telephone: "She had to keep explaining why she was panting." And Jerry, a

32-year-old printer from Milwaukee, Wisconsin, once licked his girlfriend to orgasm while they were on a night flight to Los Angeles: "I lay between her legs and covered myself up with a blanket. Every time she moaned or cried out, the flight attendant would look at her and say, 'Are you okay, miss?' and she'd have to smile, and say, 'Terrific, thank you, just having a disturbing dream.' Except it wasn't a dream, of course, it was real." Dean, a 26-year-old draftsman from Vancouver, told me, "To my mind, there's nothing better than giving a girl a face-job out in the open air. I took my girlfriend for a good long hike in the woods once, and when we were way deep among the trees, we stopped for a while and started kissing and everything. I took down her little tight hiking shorts and the little white thong she was wearing, and I knelt down in front of her and started guzzling her cunt. She just stood against this big old tree, massaging her breasts through her plaid shirt, her face held up to the sun and her eyes closed, with her shorts around her ankles and her thong halfway down her thighs while I lapped her and licked her and pushed my tongue right up inside her. In the end she had to get down on the ground because she found she couldn't have an orgasm standing up, and I spread her legs as wide as they would go and lifted them right up, and I plunged my tongue right deep in that cunt of hers and licked her some more, and it only took her four or five minutes and she came like a firecracker."

As you grow more experienced in cunnilingus—and as you grow to know your woman's sexual preferences better—you will be able to control her feelings of passion almost as exactly like a chef turning a gas flame up or down. You will be able to speed up her orgasm by flicking her clitoris faster; you will be able to slow it down by taking your tongue away from it and paying more attention to her vagina. You will find that you can keep up regular flicking of the clitoris but delay orgasm by opening the lips of her vulva wider with your fingers; and you can accelerate orgasm by holding the sides of the fleshy area in which her clitoris is buried between finger and thumb (almost like holding your nose when you dive into a swimming pool) and firmly but gently massaging it as you lick its exposed tip. These techniques are not infallible. I have come across some women who climax almost immediately if their lovers stretch open their vaginal lips during cunnilingus. The idea of being so openly exposed to a man's mouth they find exquisitely arousing. Other women prefer not to have their clitoral area massaged. But these are only general guidelines to start you off, and you will soon find that you can adapt, improve, or discard any of them according to your woman's responses.

Since cunnilingus often involves additional stimulation with your fingers, let's see what your desirable digits can do to drive your woman wild in bed.

Often the insertion of a single finger into her vagina is sufficient to give her all the extra arousal she might need. Circle it around the entrance to the vagina, caress the upper lining of her vaginal barrel with a gentle beckoning motion, probe deeper into her vagina and *gently* run your fingertip around the neck of her womb.

Or, if she's very highly aroused and she obviously enjoys what you're doing, insert two fingers or three, or even more. With two fingers you can actually take hold of her womb and give it that stirring motion I referred to earlier.

When her vagina is well lubricated, you can insert your index finger into it to make it slippery and then slide it into her anus. One of the most exciting digital caresses is to insert your finger into her anus and your thumb into her vagina, and to tug and massage the intervening bridge of muscle.

An extreme form of using your fingers is "fistfucking," in which you work your entire hand up into her vagina. Few woman find this comfortable, but some find it highly exciting, especially since you can now grip her entire cervix and sensually move it. Dolly, a 28-year-old waitress from Santa Barbara, California, said: "Dave used to get turned on by doing these really far-out things with me, I guess it was almost what you might call sadomasochism except that he never used whips or chains or leather or anything like that. Just after we'd made love, he used to cram his cock and his balls and everything into my mouth; he used to make me take everything, but I can't say that I didn't like it because I did, especially if I hadn't come; it used to turn me on, too. He used to make me feel that he was using me, you know, but it wasn't cruel or vicious or anything like that, he never hurt me. Sometimes he used to fuck my bottom, he used to lie beside me while I was lying on my back, and he used to force his cock right up my ass, right up to the very hilt of it, and then he used to push his hand up my cunt, his whole hand, and take hold of his cock through the skin of my ass, and massage himself until he shot off. I mean I really felt that he was using me, but he did it on purpose, he didn't use me in any other way, and most of the time he used to make love to me quite straight, he only fucked me like that when he was feeling really horny. It hurt me at first, just a little bit, my ass and my cunt used to get sore, but only because I wasn't relaxing. When I learned to relax, it didn't hurt at all, and I used to look forward to it, I used to be able to feel him shooting his jism into my ass, and then during the night when he was sleeping I could touch my ass and feel it all sliding out of me."

It is not unknown (but not particularly recommended) for a man to fist-fuck a woman anally. The sensations are erotic and strange, but personally I advise you to let this particular variation remain a fantasy, even if it appeals to you, since it can cause damage to the anal sphincter and there is a risk of perforating the rectum, which could prove serious or even fatal.

Another strict warning about cunnilingus: You can suck and slurp at your woman's vagina as much as you like, but *never* blow into it. If you force air into a woman's uterus you can cause an air embolism that will travel around her bloodstream and kill her. There was a recorded case of a woman dying from this cause in Houston, Texas, at the end of 1985.

In all, if you treat your woman's body with respect, you will be rewarded not only with intense erotic responses, but with an appreciation from her that will outlast your first heated weeks together, and may even outlast the term of your relationship. But it is nice to know that whenever she thought of you in the future, she would always say, "Now *he* was an excellent lover."

10.
The Wilder Side of Sex

Beyond the boundaries of everyday sex that all of us know and love is a land of limitless erotic possibilities. The only restrictions to what you can do to drive your woman wild in bed are whether it's physically possible and whether you and she want to do it together.

Everybody has particular erotic tastes and fantasies. It is not abnormal to have daydreams about sexual acts and sexual situations that—if you had to explain them to somebody else out loud—would sound obscene. However, most of the grosser sexual variations that turn us on within the privacy of our own minds *remain* fantasies. In fact, they are often more arousing as fantasies than thèy are as actual acts. I have come across many men and women who have tried leather and whips and other sexual adventures and have come to the conclusion that *thinking* about them is a whole lot sexier than doing them.

Mind you, you can always share your erotic fantasies with the lady you love simply by talking about them. All you have to do is coax her to tell you what fantasies she has about making love, and then you can tell her what turns you on in return. It's surprising how many couples have no idea what their partner's most compelling erotic fantasy is all about, even though most people have a dominant fantasy that they can conjure up whenever they feel like arousing themselves.

"I used to have a fantasy about accidentally locking myself out of my house when I was naked," said Julie, a 25-year-old dancer from Sante Fe. "I went to bring in my laundry, and the door slammed, and there I was stark naked and no way to get into the house. So I had to go next door to my neighbor to get some help, but my neighbor wasn't there, just her husband and three of his friends, all big hefty guys with beer guts and fists the size of plucked turkeys. They saw me outside of the window, and came outside and stood around me, while I was trying to cover myself up because I was totally nude. Then without saying anything at all they opened up their shirts and dropped their pants and advanced on me, with their dicks all big and hard and bright red. They pinned me down on the ground, and they did just about everything to me that a man could do to a woman. They fucked me, one after the other, they jacked off all over my body, they turned me over and fucked my bottom. Then they left me lying in the dirt. Now—I'm telling you the truth—there isn't any way in the world that I'd ever want that to happen to me. But it's a turn-on to think about it. And when I told my last boyfriend about it, he picked me up and carried me out of the house and into the garage—we were both naked right there in the garage—and he dragged the blanket out of the car and laid it on the floor, and we fucked right there on the garage floor. That had all of the feeling that my fantasy had, without any of the real danger. And I guess that's the only way that you can play your fantasies out for real, by keeping all of the flavor but not actually going over the edge."

Julie's words are more than wise. If you try too hard to recreate your erotic fantasies in real life, they can become offputting or, worse than that, they can become an obsession. I am all in favor of couples playing at bondage, I am delighted to hear about couples dressing up in fantasy costumes, or making love in risky locations, such as a train or a taxi or a public park. I have encouraged dozens of couples to go out of doors to make love, or meet each other in strange motels and pretend that they are completely unknown to each other. But when games like this become *necessary* for their sexual satisfaction rather than a way of spicing up a sex life that has simply become routine, that is the time to take a long, hard look at the fundamentals of their relationship.

Most of the time, though, a creative bout of erotic play can work magic for your relationship. You are two consenting adults, there is nothing to stop you trying absolutely *everything*, from tying each other up to going to the theater stark naked under your coats.

Let's hear some of the experiences of couples who have dipped their toes into the wilder waters of sex. This is Jock, a 33-year-old auto sales manager from Newark, New Jersey: "I was always interested in what you might call the rubber scene, you know, girls dressed in black rubber outfits, with masks and all that kind of stuff. I went out with Lisa for almost a year before I mentioned it to her. There was an article in some fashion magazine about rubber dresses; apparently they were fashionable for top models and rock singers and people like that. I looked at this girl in this rubber dress, and I said, 'Jeez, Lisa, I'd love to see you in something like that,' and she said, 'Rubber?' And it must have been that third martini because I told her all about it, you know, the way I used to think about rubber, how sexy it was. And she said, 'Do you want me to try it?' And I couldn't believe what I was hearing; she was offering to wear rubber. So I shrugged and said, 'Yeah, well, you know, if you want to.' And she said, 'Do you want me to try it, give me a straight answer,' and I said yes. So I got hold of this magazine advertising rubberwear, and I sent off for the catalogue, and there was all this rubber stuff. We looked through it together, and—well, shit, I was real shy about it at first; it makes you shy when somebody suddenly discovers your fantasy—but then she said choose what you want me to wear, you know, no holds barred, I'm doing this for you. So I chose black rubber stockings, and a black rubber T-shirt that left the breasts exposed, and a pair of black rubber panties, only they weren't just panties, they had rubber dildoes inside them, one was supposed to go up the vagina and the other was supposed to go up the anus, only they were up there all the time. I didn't know how Lisa was going to react, but she said okay, and I paid my $95 or whatever the stuff cost and sent away for it. It took so long to arrive that I forgot all about it, but one day I came home from work and there was Lisa standing in the hallway. She was wearing this tight shiny black rubber top, and her bare breasts were bulging out of it and her nipples were sticking out like I'd never seen them sticking out before, or maybe it was imagination. She wore these tight black rubber panties, and her legs were completely sheathed in black rubber stockings. She was smiling at me, and she came right up to me and she put her arms around me, and she was crazy for it, I mean she really wanted it there and then, right in the hallway. But I took her through to the bedroom, and if there were world records for taking off your clothes, I'd be holding all of them. I laid her down on the bed, and I climbed on top of her, and I kissed her and held her, and she fastened her legs around me, they were all shiny and rubbery; you can't imagine the slick feel of those stockings, and the rubbery smell. I kissed her breasts and sucked her nipples; her breasts looked enormous the way they protruded out of that rubber T-shirt, white breasts against black rubber. And then I tugged down those panties, and inside them I could see those two black rubber dildoes slowly coming out of her vagina and her anus, both of them slippery and shining. I rolled them right off, those panties, and her vagina was all ready for me, all ready and hot, and I slid my cock in right where that dildo had been, and we fucked and we fucked until we didn't know what day it was. We made a night of it. We didn't even stop for dinner that night. We fucked and sucked and those rubber stockings were all shiny with sweat and spunk and saliva, and that was one of the sexiest nights ever, for both of us. Now and again, Lisa puts them on again, and I like them, but I don't insist, you know, and if she did it too often the novelty would wear off. I think that's what keeping your sex life interesting is all about, novelty."

It's interesting to note that once Jock had indulged his fantasy about rubber, it quickly lost its first appeal. Many women would be less alarmed about their lovers' sexual tastes if they understood that few men are serious fetishists, few *need* to have their women dressed in rubber in order to reach a satisfactory climax. But there is eroticism in all kinds of smells and textures and new experiences, and if you want to try rubber (or any other kind of clothing) then by all means do so. The worst that can happen is that you discover that you don't really like it after all.

If your woman expresses a strong sexual desire, you should help her to indulge that desire just as readily as you would expect her to indulge yours. In fact, 85 percent of the women I talked to said that if their husbands or lovers ever showed an interest in playing out *their* fantasies, they would be far readier to help their husbands or lovers to play out whichever fantasy appealed to them.

So, take the trouble to coax your woman into telling you what turns her on the most, and suggest that you play it out for real. It may be something as simple as video recording your lovemaking and playing it back while you make love yet again. Quite a high percentage of women said that watching themselves making love on video was "a revelation." They had never realized what they looked like during intercourse; some had never properly inspected their own vulvas before. "You feel as if you've been doing something with your eyes closed all your life," said Renee, a 36-year-old hotel receptionist from San Francisco.

Your woman's fantasy may be to have you tie her up to the bed and make love to her while she lies there unable to prevent you. One woman I talked to liked to be staked out nude on the lawn in her backyard, as if she were a sacrifice to the Apaches. Her husband would then disappear and not tell her when he was going to return. Sometimes he stayed in the house; sometimes he went for a drive. Once he went out for drinks with a friend, and left her naked and helpless on the lawn for almost three hours. "It was frightening and erotic, both at the same time. Suppose some stranger had come into the yard and found me like that? This wasn't night, remember, this was broad daylight. I would have been completely helpless, lying there nude with my legs wide apart. After a while, though, my husband comes back, and he does to me whatever he wants. It's not knowing what he's decided to do and when he's going to come back and do it that makes the whole game so arousing."

Mild bondage can be stimulating for both partners. Jackie, from Minneapolis, Minnesota, liked to handcuff her lover to the end of their brass bed and fellate him nearly to the point of climax. Then she would leave him alone for a while, so that she could come back and fellate him all over again—and again, just short of ejaculation. "I could go on for hours, time after time, and by the end he used to be begging me to bring him off, so that's when I did. He used to spray all over the room, it was unbelievable."

There are specific rules about bondage that even the severest of S/M practitioners observe.

1. Bondage must never be attempted by either partner unless both partners are in full and unconditional agreement that they want to try it.
2. Nothing must ever be fastened around the neck.
3. Breathing must never be restricted in any way at all.
4. Somebody who is tied up should never be left without supervision (a rule that our lady friend who was staked out in the yard failed to observe, to her obvious peril. Suppose a stranger *had* walked into the yard and found her?).
5. Never use knots that are difficult to undo, and never use locks unless they are quickly and easily unfastened.
6. Never attempt bondage when you have been drinking. The clarity of your judgment could be vital.
7. Before you start, agree on a "release" signal that will be honored immediately and without argument whenever it is given by either of you.

Having given all these sobering cautions, bondage can be erotic and fun. For tying up, use the pliable terylene rope supplied for yachts; it cannot be broken but it does not chafe bare skin. Also, the knots in terylene rope are easier to unfasten in a hurry than the knots in regular rope.

Once one of you is bound up, the other can do anything that he or she wants—from masturbation to oral sex to the relentless application of dildoes. Tina, a 24-year-old housewife from Sherman Oaks, California, said: "Brad used to massage me with baby oil while I was tied up naked with my hands behind my back. He used to squeeze my breasts and slide his hand between my legs, and by the time he had finished I was practically howling for it. To me, a massage just isn't the same unless I'm tied up. It's that feeling that a man can rub you all over wherever he wants to, and you can't do anything to stop him."

Some women like their men to dress up—and if your woman really wants to do it, why not oblige? This is Lavinia, a 28-year-old hairstylist from Los Angeles: "I don't know where this particular fantasy came from. But I was always turned on by the idea of seeing my husband Peter in women's underwear. It sounds real kinky, doesn't it? But I used to lie in bed and think what it would be like to be screwed by a man who was wearing women's underwear. In the end, we were on the beach one day, just walking, and I told him about it. I don't know why. Well, he was real silent for a long time, and I thought that he was angry. But after about five minutes, he said, 'Whatever turns you on. You want to do it, I don't mind, I'm game.' So we went to Frederick's and bought some sheer black stockings and a black garter belt and a black see-through G-string, and we laughed about it a lot; it was fun as well as sexy. And that night, Peter put on these stockings and garters but he couldn't fit into the G-string because his cock was sticking out so stiff. It was kinky, yes, seeing him dressed like this, but it made both of us excited. I made him go downstairs and make me a cup of coffee dressed like that, naked except for black stockings and garters. I made him lie on his back on the bed and I climbed on top of him, and fucked him at my own sweet pace. Then afterwards I insisted he sleep in his stockings. We didn't do it again, only that once. It was a strange experience but very exciting. I don't have to analyze it, do I?"

Your sexual relationships with your woman will develop and progress and deepen with every new experience you try—even if it doesn't completely work out. Many of the so-called "kinky" sexual acts are nothing more than the result of couples satisfying their curiosity about sex—tasting each other's sexual juices, exploring each other's genitals and anal passages, trying to discover what sensations arouse them the most. I find it interesting that most well-adjusted couples who have explored the outer fringes of sex have fairly quickly returned to what you might call more "conventional" lovemaking. In other words, they were experimenting to see how far they could go and, having discovered their sexual limits, have returned to the kind of lovemaking that rewards them with the greatest affection and closeness and mutual respect.

However, I do believe that you should stretch your sexual experience as far as you can. And if you take your woman with you on your experimental journey, you will both return from it with a deeper understanding of each other's sexuality. Iris, a 31-year-old secretary from New York City, told me: "I lived with Chris for four months. We did everything in bed you could think of. We were hot for each other and we fucked anywhere and everywhere, and some of the things we tried were real dirty, when you think about them. Once he fucked me when I was standing in the kitchen, making pilaf for his mother. His mother was in the living room all the time! But he lifted up my dress at the back and he stuck it up me, and he fucked me while I was stirring the rice. I sat at the dinner table making smalltalk to his mother with sperm running down my thighs. Then one day he was sitting in the tub and I stood up with one foot on one edge of the tub and the other foot on the other edge, and I lifted up my skirt and I pissed on him, right through my panties. But do you know what he did? He lifted up his face and he opened his mouth and he let me piss straight into his mouth. We were always doing things like that. But we were made for each other, like animals. We cooled down in the end. You can't go on like that forever, you don't need to go on like that forever. But we'd done everything you can think of—and do you know what we did? Well, you know already. We got married."

I am frequently asked questions about so-called water sports. These are sexual games involving urine. For some people they hold a deep erotic fascination, and there is a whole range of videos and magazines and books dealing with the subject—from "Pee Fun Lovers" to "Wet Sisters." For most couples, urinating in front of each other or *over* each other can be a highly arousing part of foreplay. It has that childish ingredient of doing something "dirty" and "forbidden." If you want to try it, by all means try it. The best location is obviously in the tub or in the shower, although some couples I have talked to like to do it out of doors. As far as actually swallowing urine is concerned, a small quantity will do no harm, since urine is sterile, although I would advise you only to try this with a partner whose health and sexual history are impeccable. As with bondage and sadomasochistic games, most couples find that water sports are something they want to try only occasionally, when the mood takes them.

This is Michaela, 25, from Chicago: "Sam and I had been living together for about a month when we first got into showers. Well, that was what we called them. We used to take a shower together in the morning before we went to work; the shower stall was right opposite the window so it was always sunny in there during the summer. One day we were standing naked in the shower together and I started to soap Sam's cock, real slow and sensual, and it started to stiffen up. But then he said, 'I have to take a leak. I have to get out of the shower.' But I said, 'Why, I don't mind, take a leak if you want to.' So he did, and I was fascinated by the way it came spurting out of him all hot and steaming, and I held my hand in front of him so that he peed through my fingers. A couple of days later when we were showering, I asked him whether he wanted to take another leak. He said no, but I said, go on, just for me. So he did, and I knelt down in the shower stall right in front of him and held his cock so that he sprayed all over my breasts. After that it became a regular game. I used to let him do it all over my face and hair and everywhere, and sometimes I used to do it to him. We stopped doing it after a couple of months just because we got tired of it, and we wanted to try something new. No, I don't think there's anything wrong in it. It was exciting at the time. I think if you needed to do it every single time, then you'd have a problem. But it was only a game. We were just like a couple of kids, which most lovers are."

Linda Lovelace recommended the sensation of a man urinating up inside a woman's vagina; and one of the women I interviewed for this book said that her husband enjoyed her releasing herself whenever she reached a climax. A number of people also enjoy the sensation of having an enema, but this is not a sexual variation that I would particularly advise you to try with a new girlfriend.

The best ways of driving your woman wild in bed are those ways that are warm, wholehearted, and creative. Think of having sex with her not as one isolated incident of physical coupling but as a whole day or evening out. Start your act of love by making her feel good, with flowers, with a small gift (whether you've been married for twenty years or not), and with plenty of honest compliments. Make her feel good, make her understand how much you want her and how much you care for her.

Be sexually imaginative. Make love to her in the dining room for a change; or take her out to a beauty spot and make love to her in the backseat of your automobile. Book a night at a strange hotel, take her for dinner, and then take her to bed. Treat her like a goddess, treat her like a slave. But concentrate on filling her imagination with arousing feelings and erotic images.

This is Eddie, a 33-year-old construction engineer from San Diego: "I felt that our sex life was getting kind of jaded. So what I did was to take Jill out to dinner at a hotel on the bay, and during dinner I had the maître d' bring in some orchids for her. Then after dinner I told her I had a surprise. I took her up in the elevator, right to the penthouse suite, and I opened up the door, and there was the honeymoon suite just waiting for us, with flowers and champagne, and a new pearl necklace lying on the bed. It wasn't her birthday or anything, it was just a day like any other. I told her that this was *her* evening, because she was so terrific, and that I would do anything she wanted. All she actually said was, 'Make love to me.' But I undressed her, and laid her on the bed, and I told her, 'You're the princess, I'm your slave, it's my duty to give you as many orgasms as I can.' I kissed her, and fondled her, and then I went down between her legs and licked her. She was a little bit drunk from champagne, and she was crying out and moving her legs around but I wouldn't let her go. I licked her and licked her until she reached an orgasm, and then I kept on licking her and she had a second orgasm, and then a third. You have to understand that I'd never tried anything like that before, but just for this evening I was devoting myself to her pleasure, to her pride, to her body. I made love to her then, as slowly as I could, long slow strokes, and she said, 'I want to sit on top of you,' so I rolled over and she sat on top of me, and she moved herself up and down and squeezed those muscles inside of herself, and in the end I knew that I wasn't going to be able to keep from coming for very much longer. It felt like my balls were exploding inward—what do they call that, *imploding*. But immediately she straddled my chest and said, 'You're going to lick me all over again,' and she held her pussy open with her fingers and held it up my mouth. I started licking her again, and the sperm and the juice were running out of her pussy down my chin. It took her only about a half a minute to have another orgasm, and after that she lay back on the bed and she was exhausted. I held her in my arms and let me tell you something we felt closer together then than we had done for months, maybe even years. During the night I made love to her again while she was still half asleep, and before they brought up the breakfast I masturbated her with my fingers and then made love to her one more time. We left that honeymoon suite feeling like honeymooners, I can tell you, sore and satisfied. All right, it cost money, but how much money do you spend on two or three ordinary dinners and a few bunches of roses when you could be spending it on one evening like that? You're talking about wild in bed? I drove my wife wild in bed, and she wasn't just a wife, she was a sensual, beautiful woman, with a terrific body and all the passion to match. And anybody could do it. Anybody, at any time."

It was Eddie's appreciation of the fact that driving your woman wild in bed begins long before you reach the bedroom door that made his evening out with Jill such a sexual and emotional success. Women relish sex just as much as men do; and they can respond to the quick "zipless" fuck, as Erica Jong described it in her novel *Fear of Flying*. But if you want to drive her *really* wild in bed, if you want her to reach the limits of erotic pleasure, you have to start by arousing her feelings long before you start twiddling with her clitoris. Even the quick ardent act of intercourse in dangerous or exciting circumstances will only succeed if it occurs within the context of a pleasurable and arousing relationship. That relationship need not have been going on for very long. Sometimes a few minutes is sufficient, but you have to have made contact with her personality before your sexual success is 100 percent guaranteed.

The ways in which you can drive your woman wild in bed are limited only by your own imagination. But here are six women describing their peak moments of erotic pleasure, the moments when their lovers or husbands made them feel, in the words of one woman, "like the whole universe was splitting apart."

Annie, 19, from Mill Valley, California: "Keith picked me up at the local bookstore, which also serves as a coffeehouse and bus station and general meeting place for the whole community. He didn't live in Mill Valley, he was visiting a friend, but he'd come into the bookstore just to browse around. I guess you could say that our eyes met across the crowded shelves. He said hi and I said hi and we started talking. I liked him instantly. You could never say that he was handsome but he had a way of looking at me that made me feel relaxed. I don't know, he was always smiling and easygoing and he had this dry sense of humor that made me laugh. I always fall for men who make me laugh. He said he was cooking lasagne for lunch and would I like to join him, he always made too much. I said sure. So we bought a big bottle of cheap red wine and went back to his friend's house. His friend was in San Francisco for the day. He baked the lasagne and we drank wine and talked, and when lunch was ready, we took it out on to the veranda in the sunshine. He looked around and said, 'This is idyllic, a good cheap lunch, a good cheap bottle of red wine, and the prettiest girl I think I've ever seen.' I don't know. There was a magic about that day. We went for a long walk after lunch, and he wanted to know all about me; he kept the magic going because he was always funny and always interested. We held hands, and then he put his arm around my waist, and then we stopped right in the middle of nowhere at all and he kissed me. He said, 'Nobody in my whole life ever had an effect on me like you do.' We went back to his friend's house, and he poured some more wine and we kissed some more, and then he spread an Indian blanket out on the veranda, just where the sun was shining. He kissed me and unbuttoned my shirt. I don't usually wear a bra, and when he opened up my shirt, he cupped my bare breasts in his hands and he stroked my nipples and he gave me feelings that went all the way down to the soles of my feet. He unfastened my belt and slipped off my jeans and kissed me here and there and every place you could think of. Then he took off his own clothes and tossed them into the garden and laughed. He was very lean and fit and his cock stood out like a great big club. We lay down on the Indian blanket in the sunshine and he kissed me and stroked me all over. He said I was bliss, I was absolute bliss, and he caressed my breasts until I felt that I could hardly stand him caressing them any longer. Then he ran his hands down inside my thighs, and that really made me shiver. When he touched my vagina he did it so gently, he ran a single finger down it, and it was then that I felt the warm wind blowing on the wetness of it. He leaned over me, and opened me up with his fingers, and very very slowly slid his cock into me, so slowly that I wanted to punch him and tell him to push it right in, and quick. He made love to me with such grace and rhythm, and all the time he kept telling me how he was feeling, what I was doing to him, and because he was turned on I was turned on even more. My orgasm came when I was least expecting it. I suddenly found that my eyes kept wincing, and the whole day seemed to go dark. I couldn't think where I was for a moment, all I could feel was his stiff cock sliding in and out of me, that seemed to be the center of everything. Then I shouted out loud, even though I didn't realize that I did, and a feeling hit me that I can't even describe to you. I jumped around so much that his cock came out of me, and his white sperm shot out all over my stomach and my pubic hair. I remember lying there afterwards looking at him, just looking at him, and the feeling of his cum slowly drying in the sunshine on my stomach. It still gives me funny feelings. Funny *good* feelings."

The bucolic simplicity of this encounter belies the careful and appreciative way Annie's newfound friend Keith created an atmosphere that was friendly, romantic, humorous, and sexy. He never once broke the idyllic spell that had been cast by the day, by the circumstances of their meeting, and by his own good nature. Annie remained entranced by him, and he was able not only to make love to her, but to give her the most memorable sexual experience of her (admittedly young) life. She will probably meet another man whose sexual attentions will impress her even more, but for now Keith's seduction stands as her best yet, and as a classic example of how the high excitement of sexual intercourse can begin at first meeting. The sexual act is not a separate part your relationship with your woman; it's not a distinctly different activity like washing the car or going out and chopping logs. It's integral to everything you do together; it's a continuation of how you talked to her at breakfast, what you said when you called her from work, the kind of mood you were in when you met her this evening. The good lover is making love to his woman all the time, day and night, and he regards the act of intercourse as a stimulating peak in that constant lovemaking, the physical expression of a continuous process. So many women feel that "he fucks me, and then he ignores me," or "he's only interested in me when he's horny." A lot of the time that isn't true. But the men they're talking about are not taking the trouble to *show* their women that it isn't true. They react with shock and surprise when they are accused of being emotionally neglectful. Yet a little more talk, a little more interest, and a whole lot more bread-and-butter day-to-day understanding would make all the difference. Not just to the fundamental structure of their relationships, either. A relationship that is communicative and affectionate and full of mutual interest is almost always a relationship in which the sexual experience is extremely intense. Understanding brings closeness. Closeness brings better sexual arousal. Better sexual arousal brings heightened satisfaction.

This is Sophie, 29, an advertising-space seller from New York City: "Richard always seemed to be highly sophisticated. I met him at Sotheby Parke Bernet when I was attending a sale. Richard was buying furniture for the company he works for; they rent antiques to prestige offices. He was beautifully dressed in a grey double-breasted suit, he was good-looking and thoroughly at ease. He was confident too. He saw me and smiled. Then later he came over and said, 'You were quite right not to bid for that bow-fronted sideboard. It was very heavily restored.' I said, 'I didn't bid for *anything*. I only came here to watch.' And he said, 'I know, but I had to think of some way of flattering you, apart from telling you how pretty you are.' Well, I couldn't resist a line like that, could I? He invited me to have a cocktail with him, and we went to the bar at P.J. Clarke's. Then he said he had tickets for the theater that Friday, and the reason he'd wanted to talk to me was because I was the first person he'd seen that he really wanted to go with. I took a little persuading, but he seemed so charming that in the end I said yes. And the evening was marvelous. We had dinner, we went to the theater, and afterwards he took me home. I didn't invite him up. I kissed him, but I was quite firm. I have a rule not to go to bed with any man until the fourth date; and you'd be surprised how often that rule saves me from some pretty terrible relationships. He said he understood, and we arranged to meet for lunch that weekend. Do you know something—all the time he was so courteous and charming and knowledgeable. He knew about furniture, he knew about music, he knew about architecture, he knew about politics. He made me feel I was entering a whole new world. But at the same time, he was always interested in what I had to say, if I said I hated something for such-and-such a reason, he'd say, 'Well, you're right to hate it, but this is a better reason for hating it.' I guess by the fourth date I'd already made up my mind that I wanted him to take me to bed. He came around, and he brought me flowers. I said, 'This is the famous fourth date.' And Richard said, 'I know. But before you make up your mind whether you want to sleep with me or not, I want to show you something.' He had his car outside, he didn't usually bring his car. It was a BMW, very smart. He drove me downtown and then right across the Brooklyn Bridge. Then he took me around this shabby neighborhood, and finally he stopped the car outside a rundown public school with its walls all covered in graffiti. I said, 'You're trying to tell me something.' He said, 'Yes, this is where I was born, this is where I was educated. If you sleep with me tonight, the man you're going to have in bed with you isn't a Dartmouth man, or anything like it. What I am is what I made myself.' When I think about it now, what Richard did was very astute and very sexy. It was the revelation of what he really was that turned me on to him. He explained his background and his personal achievements all in one short drive around the block, and he made me feel that he wanted me to be part of it. *That* was sexy. We drove back to Manhattan and Richard said, 'I thought we'd eat in tonight.' We went back to his apartment in the Village, and there was this beautiful candlelit dinner for two all laid out. Smoked trout, beef bourguignon, salad, with beautiful wine. We ate, and we drank wine, and we listened to cello music. Afterwards, we were sitting on the couch, and he kissed me, and I kissed him back, but instead of undressing me, he slowly stripped off his own clothes until he was completely naked. It was very exciting, very arousing. Here I was, fully dressed, with a completely naked man. He slid his hand into the front of my dress, inside my bra, and caressed my nipples. Then he lifted up my dress, and drew off my panty hose. I don't usually wear panties when I wear panty hose, so when he did that I was naked under my dress. He stroked my thighs and all around my pussy; then he slipped a finger up inside me. As you can imagine, I was already turned on. I kissed him, and said, 'Let's go to bed,' but he said, 'No, let's do it here, now.' And he lifted my dress up further, and he opened up my legs, and he pushed himself into me, not roughly, but with great assurance, all the way up to the very hilt, as if he were really taking possession of me. That was what excited me so much, I think, that he had the confidence to make love to me while he was naked and I was still dressed. I can remember closing my eyes and feeling him sliding in and out of me. On each stroke he took his penis completely out, and my pussy of course got more and more slippery. Sometimes he paused for a moment when he took it out, and I almost felt a sense of panic, in case he didn't push it back in again. The back of my dress was soaked. He clutched my breasts through my dress: I could feel how close he was to coming. I reached down between my legs and his balls were tight and hard and wrinkled, beautiful. He reached down himself and our fingers intertwined, his fingers around my pussy and my fingers encircling his cock; and then he slipped one finger down and caressed my anus with his fingertip, and I reached down there, too. He worked his finger around and around, and it was slippery with all of our juice, and he pushed it up inside my bottom. I touched and stroked his finger, feeling it right up inside my anus, and then I crooked my own finger and pushed it up there right beside his, so that *both* of us had a finger up my bottom. I can still remember the feeling of that climax. It was like floating on your back in some huge warm ocean, and every now and then a wave makes you rise up and down, and all of a sudden there are more waves, and you know that a really huge wave is coming and you won't be able to do anything about it. Richard began to thrust himself into me deeper, not taking his penis out anymore, and between us we wriggled our fingers deeper and deeper, until they were completely buried inside me. Then he tugged his finger one way, and I tugged mine the other, stretching it, and he pushed another finger in, and then the wave came, and I didn't know what was happening. I opened my eyes and felt Richard shaking in my arms; shaking! And what it was, he was climaxing; he'd managed to hold it back, but when I came he had to come. We lay there together on the sofa for a long time, and I said to Richard, 'Do you know when I first realized that we were going to be lovers?' and he said no. And I said, 'The very first time I set eyes on you. But I didn't know we were going to be good lovers until you showed me where you were brought up.' That's because good lovers are always honest lovers, they don't have any modesty, they don't spare each other anything. Not their excitements, not their disappointments. It's no good faking climaxes. The only climax worth having is a real one. No relationship can ever recover from lies, or from pretending, or from anything else but the absolute truth.'"

Maybe those aren't exactly the kind of words you would expect to read in a guide to *How to Drive Your Woman Wild in Bed*. But as I said at the beginning, respect is the key to arousing and satisfying the modern, demanding woman. Your technique is vital; your sexual knowledge is vital; your skill is vital. But—

More important than any of these is your ability to be able to give your woman a sense of confidence and trust, a feeling that you have the situation completely under control, but that her wishes and her desires are going to be honored just as much as yours. You can still give her a sense of danger, especially if you are skillful and self-possessed, but as one elegant New York career lady told me, "When it comes down to the bottom line, I still want a man who behaves like a man. I don't mind if any of my men have tears in their eyes, but I don't expect them to cry."

A good example of how one man counterbalanced the sense of security and the sense of danger was given to me by Isobel, a 32-year-old library worker from Boston, who said: "Stephen was always a marvelous lover. He used to surprise me every time we went out together. He worked in real estate. You'd think that somebody who worked in real estate would be dull but not Stephen. He was very smart; every time he took me out he was wearing a suit or a sport coat and he always looked immaculate. He was always incredibly courteous too. The kind of man who takes your coat and opens doors, not like he's trying to impress you or anything, but just *naturally*, like he wouldn't think of treating a woman any other way. That always scored points with me. But he liked to make love in risky places. I remember once he was taking an elderly couple around to look at apartments overlooking Central Park, two or three quite expensive places, and he asked me to come along with him because it was the weekend. He showed the couple around one apartment and then invited them to wander around on their own. While we were waiting for them, he led me through to one of the bedrooms, and he started to kiss me, and lift up my skirt, and slide his hands into the back of my panties. I tried to argue but he wouldn't stop, and of course if I'd screamed or anything, the old couple would have heard me. He opened his pants and his cock was sticking out so hard that I couldn't resist taking hold of it and squeezing it hard. And it smelled just like *cock*, you know, clean but slightly—what do you call it?—aromatic. I knelt down and I took hold of his cock in my mouth and sucked it and licked it, and then I said, 'Come on, let's finish this later, when we've got the time.' But Stephen said 'No, I want to fuck you now,' and he turned me around so that I was facing the wall, and he said, 'Come on, hands against the wall, just like they do in detective movies.' And I put my hands flat against the wall and stood there with my bottom right out, and he lifted up my skirt and tugged my panties halfway down my thighs and he fucked me right there, standing up, and we could hear this old couple in the next room saying how pleasant the view was, and what about the fireplace, and all that kind of stuff. I had an orgasm. The sheer danger of it gave me an orgasm. I don't think I've ever had one so quickly. Stephen slipped out of me because I was jumping around so much, and he came all over the back of my legs and into my outstretched panties. The old couple came into the room and Stephen had to turn around and pretend he was looking out of the window while he discreetly zippered up his pants. I managed to pull my panties up but of course they were all splattered with Stephen's cum. Not that I minded. Later on, when we were looking around the next apartment, I went to the bathroom and put my fingers down into my panties and I could smell him, that real strong masculine smell of him. That was what always made him so attractive, his spontaneity. If he felt like making love to me, he would, right away, and he would always leave me feeling like a woman. And not just an ordinary woman either. A very special woman."

Compare these real interviews with real women with the fictitious stories you read in books and magazines. They're not "panting for it" the way they are in fiction—even though they're strongly interested in sex and eager for sexual satisfaction. They want much more than just an erect penis with legs and billfold too. They want the kind of man that you can be—that you always *have* been, potentially.

I can give you no more confidence now than to say that your time has come. From today— from the moment you close this book—you are going to get out there and find and impress the woman you want. You are going to drive your woman wild in bed.

11.
Fifty Ways to Turn Your Woman on Tonight

Here are some suggested ways to excite the lady in your life this evening. You can choose which of these titillations you think she might enjoy, but don't be hesitant about taking one or two risks. Nothing ventured, nothing gained.

When you've tried a particular technique, make a note of how she felt about it. You don't have to write an epic. "*Ooohhhhhh*" will do.

1. Telephone her at work and tell her how much you want to take her clothes off and make slow passionate love to her.
2. Pick her up at work, take her straight home, and straight into the bedroom.
3. Arrange to meet her at an unfamiliar hotel. Tell her that you'll be waiting for her in room 303, naked.
4. Invite her out for dinner, but insist that she wear stockings and garters and no panties.

5. During dinner, discreetly slide your hand up her skirt.

6. Bathe her, soaping her as intimately as you like.

7. Dry her, and shower her with talc. Then take her to bed and give her cunnilingus until she reaches an orgasm.

8. Give her cunnilingus while she's sitting on the couch watching TV.

9. Ask her to wear stockings and high-heeled shoes to bed.

10. Ask her what her strongest erotic fantasy is, and offer to play it out for her.

11. Tie her wrists and her ankles with scarves, and rouse her to orgasm without having intercourse with her.

12. Kiss her, lingeringly, all over.

13. Suggest that she tie you up and do anything she likes with you.

14. Take her out into your backyard (or anywhere secluded in the open air) and make love to her under the stars.

15. Give her cunnilingus immediately after intercourse, until she reaches another orgasm.

16. Tell her you love her.

17. Let her hold your penis while you urinate.

18. Take her out dancing. Hold her close and tell her how much you want to make love to her.

19. Cover your bed in fresh-cut flowers.

20. Have a crackling fire and a bottle of champagne ready for her when she comes home.

21. Tell her all about your most arousing erotic fantasy.

22. Take a home-video of your woman naked. Tell her to let herself go, to express herself any way she likes. Then make love to her while you play it back.
23. Ask her to show you how she likes to have her clitoris caressed.
24. Caress it for her, until she climaxes.
25. Slide your fingers into her vagina, and give her the internal massage of her life.
26. Kiss and caress her breasts for at least five minutes.
27. Buy yourself some smart new designer underwear.
28. Buy yourself some smart new clothes.
29. Write her a letter, mostly romantic but also a little bit erotic, telling her how much your life has changed since you met her.
30. Buy her perfume, a necklace, any unexpected gift. Make it expensive. Send it for no reason at all except that she turns you on.
31. Buy her some beautiful silky underwear.
32. Give her an allover massage with scented oil. Pay special attention to her breasts and to her vulva. Don't make love to her unless she asks you to.
33. Make love to her at unexpected times. Halfway through the afternoon. Out driving in the country. At work, anywhere. Don't take *ulp!* for an answer.
34. Rent an erotic video and watch it together with a bottle of good red wine.

35. Shave, shower, and be waiting for her when she comes back from work, wearing nothing but a towel.

36. Leave your office halfway through the day, drive home, and make love to her.

37. Ask her to shave off her pubic hair.

38. Shave off yours.

39. Make a deal that whatever she asks you to do sexually, you'll do. And, in return, she has to do whatever you ask.

40. Make yourself late for work; make love to her one more time before you leave.

41. Make love in front of a mirror.

42. Ask her to masturbate herself to orgasm so that you can watch. Tell her that you'll do the same for her.

43. Buy her something personal that you know she's always wanted. A painting, a book, a record, an exercise cycle, whatever.

44. Wake her up first thing in the morning by licking her vulva.

45. Ask to watch her taking a pee.

46. Take her to a topless joint or a strip club.

47. Drive her someplace quiet and make love to her in the back of the car, just like you used to.

48. Dip your cock in champagne and ask her if it improves the flavor.

49. Kiss her and caress her and see how many orgasms you can give her.

50. Tell her you love her. Tell her that she turns you on.

You are bound to have sexy games of your own that you can play. But these fifty are just a beginner's list to start you off. When you try them, be confident and straightforward about them. Sexual games are nothing to be ashamed of. Nor is natural curiosity about your woman's body and her erotic responses.

There is a whole world of exciting sex waiting for you. My only advice to you now is: Don't read, make love! And drive your woman wild in bed.

Author's note:

For obvious reasons of personal privacy, I have changed the names of the men and women who consented to have their interviews appear in this book. Other inconsequential details have been altered where there might be a risk of identification. I wish to thank all those who generously gave their time, their interest, and some of their very personal stories so that all of us could learn more about the pleasures of sex.

Graham Masterton

HOW TO DRIVE YOUR MAN WILD IN BED

For the ultimate in sexual pleasure

Star

Graham Masterton

HOW TO BE THE PERFECT LOVER

And fulfil your wildest dreams

HOW TO GET MORE OUT OF SEX

THAN YOU EVER THOUGHT YOU COULD

In writing *How to Get More Out of Sex* Dr Reuben has drawn on current medical and psychiatric literature, on consultations with other professionals in the field of human relations, and on his own experience as a psychiatrist to produce a book that, first and foremost, will help YOU.

David Reuben MD

A sympathetic and
comprehensive analysis of
female sexual problems
Robert Chartham

advice to
WOMEN

advice to
MEN

A penetrating analysis
of male sexual problems
Robert Chartham